Talking
So People
Will Listen

Women of Confidence Series

The Women of Confidence series is designed to help women confidently express their God-given gifts in every facet of their intellect, personality, style, and talents. All women have things they wish they could do better—or do at all. Those things may be something practical and close to home—like learning to communicate—or they could be something to fortify the soul, like praying. This series has it all.

Written by respected Christian communicators and authors, the Women of Confidence series helps women find new ways to live enthusiastically and confidently in the light of God's love.

OTHER BOOKS IN THE SERIES

A Confident, Dynamic You
Ten Keys to Moving From I Can't to I Can
MARIE CHAPIAN

A Woman of Strength
Reclaim Your Past, Seize Your Present, and Secure Your Future
NEVA COYLE

Empowered by Choice
Positive Decisions Every Woman Can Make
KENDRA SMILEY

The 500 Hats of a Modern Day Woman
(available February 1999)
JOYCE ELLIS

Money and Me
(available February 1999)
CYNTHIA YATES

Women of Confidence
SERIES

Talking
So People
Will Listen

Florence *and*
Marita Littauer

SERVANT PUBLICATIONS
ANN ARBOR, MICHIGAN

Vine Books is an imprint of Servant Publications especially designed to serve evangelical Christians.

Unless otherwise noted, Scripture quoted in this book is from the King James Bible.

Personal names have been used throughout this book with the permission of the individuals named.

Published by Servant Publications
P.O. Box 8617
Ann Arbor, Michigan 48107

02 03 04 05 11 10 9 8 7

Printed in the United States of America
ISBN 1-56955-081-6

LIBRARY OF CONGRESS CATALOGING-IN-PUBLICATION DATA

Littauer, Florence, 1928-
Talking so people will listen / Florence and Marita Littauer.
    p.   cm. — (Women of confidence series)
Includes bibliographical references.
ISBN 1-56955-081-6 (alk. paper)
1. Communication.   I. Littauer, Marita.   II. Title.   III. Series.
P90.L477   1998
302.2—dc21   98-11847
                                                             CIP

Contents

Preface

FLORENCE

M y "Silver Box" message started out as a spontaneous children's sermon where we looked at our words as a gift: a little silver box with a bow on top. As I give this message today based on Ephesians 4:29, I begin by giving the audience the verse and then helping them to apply the Scripture to their own lives:

"Let no corrupt communication proceed out of your mouth, but that which is good to the use of edifying, that it may minister grace unto the hearers." Children look up wide-eyed at all those big words but I share that we will take the verse apart and make it easy to understand.

Let's start with the word *mouth*. "We all know what a mouth is," I tell them. "Now let's see, what comes out of it. Here it's called communication. What is communication?"

When I ask that question, children call out "talking."

"That's right, but if I locked myself in a closet and talked all afternoon, would I be communicating?"

They shake their heads "no."

"Why not?"

"Nobody's listening."

"Is that the way it is at your house—everyone's talking and no one's listening?"

"Oh, yes," they exclaim, "that's the way it is at our house!"

As we all smile over the children's point of view, I explain that nearly all of us can talk, but few of us communicate. We don't truly communicate until someone listens and cares about what we say. Why don't people seem to care? Are we answering questions no one has asked? Are we repeating the same message over and over so people tune us out? Are we babbling on endlessly without giving others a chance to talk? Are we telling stories that don't fit into the conversation? Are we jumping in with interruptions that we think are more interesting than what others have to say?

Communication is a two-way street. It's not always the other person's fault when communication fails. Sometimes *we* are to blame because we've never learned the difference between talking and communicating. Our schools didn't teach us and our parents became our examples—not always good examples. If our parents yelled at each other, we may tend to do the same thing with our husbands. If Father barked orders and Mother dutifully went along, stuffing her hurt feelings under her apron, we may tend to think that's how good women behave. If our mothers cried plaintively to get our fathers' attention, we may think tears are an effective tool of communication. So much of our understanding comes from our childhood experiences and few of us women have thought seriously about how we can communicate more effectively, whether it's one-on-one, one to a family, one to a group, or one to hundreds from a platform. No matter what level of exchange you wish to improve upon or what aspirations you might have for your future, we hope that this book will help you, even inspire you, to move onward and upward. All of us can talk, but few of us know how to communicate.

Introduction

How Can We Improve Our Communication Skills?

∾

FLORENCE

Nido R. Qubein, past president of the National Speakers Association, came to this country from Lebanon with no money but an eager desire to learn the language and become a success. From menial jobs, where he out-performed Americans who knew English, Qubein rose higher and higher until today he is a successful man who teaches executives how to improve their communication skills. He is so grateful for what this country has allowed him to become that he has established numerous charities, which he funds liberally, to give back some of what he has received.

How did he become a success? If I had been dropped into Lebanon with no money or language skills, what would I have done? What would you have done? In his book *How To Be A Great Communicator*, Nido Qubein spells out his five steps to effective communication.

1. Desire to Improve

In my years of speaking to and counseling thousands of women, I have learned that, without a strong desire to change on the part of the individual seeking help, even the best advice will be worthless. If you go to the doctor with a malady and he knows exactly what to prescribe for your case but you never take the medicine, his wisdom is of no avail. Without the desire to improve, nothing happens.

Many people come to us looking for assistance, and we have learned to give them an assignment, a book to read, a tape to listen to, and then to tell them to give our office a call when they have completed the work. Few call. Why? They want instant answers, they want to talk about the problem, and they want sympathy, but few want to do something that takes commitment on their part. Without a serious desire to change, nothing much happens. Because you are reading this book, we know you are an above-average person who has already made a decision to improve your communication skills. You have an advantage over Nido Qubein: you know the language.

2. Understand the Process

Communication is not just a steady, easy flow of words, but an ability to create complete pictures with your words. Qubein says we must learn to "translate the images and sounds we receive through our eyes and ears into words that will inform and inspire others."

In the CLASSeminar we call this step "Verbal Visuals" and give examples that people can see. Make your sentences specific, using words that are clear rather than vague. Not "A lady once said to me," but "As I stood on the steps of a small country church, a tall blonde lady who looked like a model approached me and said ..." What a difference in interest when we communicate in such a way that people can see what we're saying.

At the CLASSeminar I ask the participants to picture a ten-drawer filing cabinet. Then I ask them what they saw. The answers are amazing as they each describe their personal creation. Some are oak, some mahogany, some steel. Some have little drawers, some are normal size, and some are lateral files. Some have the ten drawers stacked vertically, reaching to the ceiling, some have two sets of five each, and some create five sets of two each. One confused lady had three sets of three and said, "But I didn't know what to do with the extra drawer so I threw it away." We've even had altercations over these personal creations: when a young man from New Zealand told of his lateral files with colored folders, a scrappy lady behind him called out, "That's my idea! You can't have my file drawers!" What we have learned is that we all have creative minds that can instantly build a file cabinet (or anything else) by the mere suggestion of a word, and we can do it faster than a Polaroid camera.

To communicate effectively, give people the opportunity to see what you are saying. Dress your principles in personality. Be creative and colorful. Keep the audience's interest by challenging them to build the message along with you.

3. Master Basic Skills

Building a large vocabulary is a basic skill largely ignored by most people. As long as they get their point across, most people pay little attention to the words they use to achieve their goal. Many speakers are boring because they constantly repeat simple words. Things are good or bad, big or little, near or far. The point of increasing our vocabulary is not to impress people with our brilliance, but to be accurate and clear. The word *big* is very weak when describing a towering building, a vast expanse, an overwhelming fear. We need the correct word to express each different idea. Qubein says that our aim should be to convey messages people can understand and to connect with the listeners so they won't tune us out. When I read that, I immediately erected a verbal visual. I pictured each person I met as carrying a TV remote control in his pocket. If I didn't hold his attention he could quietly change channels with the flick of a switch. I would be gone and his mind could be off to McDonald's or the football game.

How many of you can sense when people click you off? Are they just being rude, or are you not communicating effectively? I need to remember that TV clicker that everyone has hidden in his mind. My job will be to make sure the listener doesn't change channels.

4. Practice

Do we listen to ourselves and try to improve our communication skills? Do we ask our children how well we express ourselves to them and then listen to their answers? How much we can learn from asking questions of honest people who are dying to give us their opinion! Perhaps the best way of all to improve our skills is to tape-record everything we present to others, including some dinner table conversation. Listening to ourselves is difficult, sometimes shocking, but hearing is believing. We can hear our repetitions of certain words, our dropping the *g* off "-ing" words, the monotone of our voice, or our lack of enthusiasm. Once we've overcome the thought, "Surely I don't really sound like that!" the next step is video. The camera is heartless, shows every flaw in word and clothing, and is rarely flattering! Yet, when taken to heart, a video of yourself is worth a thousand words. You don't need to watch yourself in a mirror when you can practice before a video camera.

5. Have Patience

None of us improves overnight, but if we aren't trying, we won't improve at all. In fact, our bad habits get worse as we get older. Remember the expressions, "Rome wasn't built in a day" and "If you don't know where you're going, any road will get you there." We need to develop a plan for where we're going, do something to achieve our goal, practice our skills, and try to speed up the process.

Using Qubein's points as a basis and then applying them to our own lives, I hope I've challenged you to read on. We, as women, need to work at improving our communication skills, whether we wish to be effective at home, in the business world, in social relationships, or in front of a larger audience.

Part One

❧

The Four Personalities

one .

Discovering Your
Communication Personality

∾

MARITA

Have you noticed there are people out there who are different from you? Chances are you probably live with, work with, or have at some time associated with someone who responds to life quite differently from the way you do. These differences are what make us unique individuals and give us our own customized personalities. Our personalities are the filter, or colored glasses, through which we view life. They affect nearly every aspect of our lives—even the way we communicate.

My husband Chuck and I had been married about three years when the way we communicate because of our personalities became quite clear. Because we are such opposites, we even use a totally different vocabulary. My words are colorful. Exciting. Spoken in extremes. Chuck employs the "need to know" law. If you don't *need* to know it, he won't say it.

One weekend morning, I cooked Chuck a special breakfast. This was not just Pop-Tarts and Tang. I went all out. I made fresh, homemade buttermilk pancakes—not from a mix, bacon, freshly-ground coffee, and freshly-squeezed orange juice. I served it in the dining room on our good china with coordinating linens. I set the extraordinary breakfast in front of Chuck and he began to eat it. I asked him how his breakfast was and he answered, "Fine."

FINE! I thought to myself. *I make this great meal and all it is, is FINE?*

Chuck was communicating to me out of his personality and I was hearing him from mine. Later in this chapter I'll describe the four basic personality types. As I survey audiences when I speak, I find that those who have the Popular Sanguine personality—like mine—universally view the word *fine* as a negative. I ask them, "On a scale of one to ten, with ten being the best, where is the word *fine?*" In unison they shout out answers ranging from one to three. (Once, someone said "minus two!") However, a Perfect Melancholy sees things differently.

On one of my frequent speaking trips, I called home as I always do. I asked Chuck how his day had been and he responded with a predictable "Fine." Without thinking I said, "What was wrong?" "Nothing," he replied, "I said it was fine. You need to learn that for me, fine is as good as it ever gets."

For the two of us opposite personalities to communicate, and ultimately stay married, we have needed to learn to communicate *for* each other. Chuck has learned to add superlatives to his speech. "Terrific!" "Fabulous!" "Wonderful!" "Amazing!" If I have a new dress and I ask him how I look, he has learned that "fine" is not an acceptable answer! When I ask Chuck about something in his life and he says it is "fine," I have learned to reply "great," and move on to the next subject.

On the day when I served Chuck the lavish breakfast and he said it was fine, I said "wrong answer" as I took his plate back to the kitchen. I turned around and brought it back, placed it in front of him, and asked, "Chuck, how's your breakfast?" With a big smile on his face he said, "This is the *best* breakfast I have ever had in my *entire* life!"

"Good," I replied, "now you can have breakfast tomorrow."

What is Your Communication Personality?

Each of us has a primary personality, and most of us have a strong secondary type. Prepackaged with what we are comes a built-in communication style. Some of us can talk incessantly, whether or not anyone is interested or listening. Some of us are good at quick commands, keeping conversation to "just the facts, Ma'am. Just the facts." Others are better at listening than talking, sharing only on a "need-to-know" basis. As listeners, some prefer to stay uninvolved and are almost fearful to enter into a conversation. Yet in a time of stress, they are the ones to talk to: just the sound of their voices alone is calming.

Each communication personality has areas of great strength—areas where it naturally excels. Additionally, each personality has areas that need improvement.

First we are going to discover your own communication personality and its unique areas of strength. We will examine aspects of your personality that may need some adjustment in order for you to communicate effectively with others. In the next chapter we will offer valuable suggestions on how you can modify your approach to people whose communication personalities do not match yours. You will learn to identify the communication style of those with whom you live and work and to adjust your approach to them so you can communicate more effectively.

The Personalities

There are four basic personalities. While none of us fit exactly into one "type," we each have a built-in framework that is our personality. The great Greek philosophers first observed these four personalities more than two thousand years ago. Hippocrates noticed that people were different, and gave them specific designations based on their primary personality traits. Today his original teaching has been added to and updated, but the original concepts have proven themselves over and over throughout the ages.

The Popular Personality

Hippocrates called those persons who are easiest to identify, Sanguines. Another name for this personality type is the "Popular personality," and we will use that terminology in this book. Their loud speech, easy laugh, and expressive body language make these people easy to spot. Often when I speak on this subject, individuals are able to identify their own popular personality or that of friends just on the word *loud*. In short, the Popular person is the talker of life.

The Perfect Personality

The next easiest to identify is the Melancholy personality, also called the "Perfect Personality." While the Popular personality has an open mouth, an open life, and open gestures, the

Perfect personality is just the opposite. Her mouth is closed: she speaks only when she really has something to contribute. Her life is closed: she shares few of her thoughts or feelings, and then only with those to whom she is especially close. Her body language is closed: she uses few gestures as she speaks and those gestures are often in short, choppy motions. The Perfect personality prefers to think, then speak. She is the thinker of life.

The Powerful Personality

The third personality type is the Choleric or "Powerful personality." These are very busy people—and their communication often consists of commands and orders, with little time for chitchat. Their body language consists of pointing, pounding, and positioning. They are the personalities for whom the expression "in your face" was created. They often wag a finger in your face as they talk to you. When speaking to a Powerful personality, you may find yourself backing up, which will then prompt her to move forward. They also use a fist for emphasis, pounding on a desk or a wall, or may even pound both hands to make a point. They prefer to stand in a control position, with both hands on their hips as if to say, "Do what I say or get out of the way." The Powerful personality is the worker of life.

Do any of these personalities sound like anyone you know? Perhaps you've identified yourself already. These first three personalities are the easiest to identify. If none of them seems to fit so far, perhaps the next one will relate to you or someone in your life.

The Peaceful Personality

Phlegmatics—or, as we call them, "Peaceful personality" people—are mentioned last, not because they are the least important, but because they are the hardest to identify quickly. They are the people who are steady and balanced, even and consistent. They do not have the extreme traits found in the other personalities. Often they are best identified by the process of elimination. Their voice is softer, exuding a calming presence. They speak only when they have something of value to share, and they are hesitant to offer opinions. Their body language is relaxed. In contrast to the wild flailing of the Popular personality, the Peaceful uses few or no gestures. However, they can be identified by the fact that they prefer to lean on something while standing and to recline as much as possible while sitting. They are the watchers in life.

This quick overview of the personalities should help you identify your own personality. If you still do not recognize your own personality type, we suggest you read one or all of our three books, *Personality Plus, Personality Puzzle* and *Getting Along With Almost Anybody*.[1]

The Popular Personality

Known for her "gift of gab," the Popular personality can talk anywhere, at anytime, with anyone. This is a great asset in both personal and professional situations, often making this personality the life of the party. However, with these strengths come some companion weaknesses on which all Popular personalities need to work in order to communicate effectively.

Limit Conversation

The Popular personality needs to learn to limit conversation and allow others the opportunity to talk—even if what you have to say is more interesting and entertaining (at least in your own mind). Someone who talks constantly eventually becomes a bore, even when her stories are entertaining. Work on speaking only when you have something to say that people *need* to know or is vital to the situation. Like the little boy who cried wolf, the Popular personality who is always talking will not be heard when she has something of great importance to say.

Whenever I am with a Popular personality who has not worked to overcome this communication obstacle, I am reminded of a principle that I am grateful to have learned from my mother many years ago. She told me that if I were in the midst of a story or conversation and were interrupted, I should just let my story drop. If someone was really interested in hearing what I had to say, he or she would remember and urge me to continue. If no one did, there was not that much interest. This is a painful lesson for all of us who have the Popular personality.

Tone Down Voice

Remember, one of the traits of the Popular personality is a loud voice. This is a great asset if you are a public speaker in a room without a microphone. However, in most settings the loud volume is distracting, irritating, and even obnoxious to others. If you are a Popular personality, you need to learn to tone down your voice. "Be beautiful inside, in your hearts, with the lasting charm of a gentle and quiet spirit which is so precious to God" (1 Peter 3:4, LB).

I am about half Popular personality and this part of me includes a loud voice. As a speaker I always considered my voice an asset—that is, before I got married. I always have much to say. When my husband (who is a Perfect personality) and I go to a restaurant, and I begin to regale him with the events of my day, he notices that others in the restaurant are listening to my story. He shushes me, wanting me to speak more quietly. As I have surveyed audiences, I have found that I am not alone in my loud habits. Those of us who share the Popular personality like a big audience for our stories; even if that audience has no business listening, we like them to join in. I often ask my audiences, "What do we Populars do when we discover someone is listening in on our story?" Universally they shout back to me, "Talk louder!" However, just because everyone else with our personality speaks loudly, this does not make loudness a trait of effective communication.

My husband has encouraged me to notice other loud Popular personalities at parties and other social gatherings. He has helped me to see how unattractive their loud, brassy demeanors truly are, especially for women. In watching others, I have seen the need to work at toning down my own volume. Chuck and I have developed a code. When we are out in public, or even at home and I am wound up—as I become when I am excited—he simply and quietly says, "FM." This is a reminder that I need to tone down and talk like an FM deejay. When I come home from a trip where I have been a bit wound up, I practice my FM deejay voice by reading street signs and billboards in that low-key, sultry voice. While I can never really talk like that, it does help me tone down my voice.

Learn to Listen

Most of us with a Popular personality think that being quiet is the same as listening. In reality most of us are not listening, but working on our next lines. I once heard that the reason people do not remember names is because they do not care enough to listen in the first place. I was sure this was not the case for me. After all, the personality charts all say that the Popular personality can't remember names.

Therefore, I set out to disprove the theory. I decided that when I met someone new, I would repeat the name within the first few minutes of conversation. I might say something like, "Really, Kathy, how did that happen?" Unfortunately, I found that the theory was correct. More often than not, when I attempted to use the name, I could not remember it! This was not because of bad memory, it was because of poor listening!

To train myself to listen better, I humiliated myself several times by saying, "I'm sorry, what did you say your name was again?" It only took a few times of embarrassment before I learned to listen better. Once I was truly listening, I found that I am excellent at remembering names. The reason we Populars can't remember names is because we don't listen.

The Perfect Personality

If you are a Perfect personality, you need to remember that the title "Perfect" does not mean you *are* perfect, but rather that you *like* perfection. While there are many aspects of your personality that are "perfect" that others could emulate, there are still some areas where you can improve. One of those areas is communication.

Add Humor

The Perfect personality is the opposite of the Popular personality. Where the Popular personality needs to learn to listen, listening is one of the strengths of the Perfect personality. The Popular personality is naturally funny but the Perfect personality needs to work on adding humor to her communication. My friend Marilyn Heavilin told me that in her early years of speaking she thought that the Perfect personality did not really have a sense of humor. She has since found out this is not true at all.

The Perfect personality does have a wonderful sense of humor. It is a humor that will not be used to entertain, because that seems frivolous. We often see it, however, when she is teaching people a new concept. The Perfect personality's sense of humor will come through as she shares true stories about her life and family. Perfect personalities would be hard pressed if they had to start off each talk or conversation with a "joke," however. They are not natural jokesters.

Marilyn said, "I realized I could cause an audience to laugh when I shared the following story, which is total truth and no exaggeration. People still laugh. The story provides a light spot in a heavy subject.

"After the death of our son, Nathan, Glen and I were really struggling in our marriage. As I trudged home each night from teaching at the school where Nathan had attended, I often thought, 'I could probably make it through this day OK if I just didn't have to deal with that man (meaning my husband) when I get home.' I'm sure he was thinking the same about me. As time went on, our relationship worsened to the point where we were barely speaking. One night Glen got between the TV set and me. He sat right in front of me;

looked me square in the eyes; and said, 'I don't care what you do. I'm not leaving!' Well, I don't know about you, but at that point, that wasn't very good news to me! My honesty about my feelings always gets a laugh." Perfect personalities can have a wonderful sense of humor when they just speak honestly about how they deal with life. Don't force it, and don't make up stories. Just be yourself.

Another way to add humor is through jokes and funny quips. Oddly enough, most joke tellers are Perfect personality types, not Populars. The Popular personalities can't remember punch lines! Jay Leno is a Perfect. He plans, rehearses, and re-rehearses the delivery of his comedy routine. Gary Larson is a wonderful Perfect personality cartoonist. Learn to look at life through his Far Side filter. I find that most of my Perfect personality friends love his work, while I can't understand half of his cartoons!

Remember to smile when you are speaking and to laugh at other people's humor as well. As Reinhold Niebuhr said, "Humor is the prelude to faith, and laughter is the beginning of prayer." Even the most serious personality will benefit from a light touch!

Enter Into the Conversation

Since the Perfect personality is naturally a listener and not a talker, she needs to work at participating in the conversation. It is very easy for the Perfect personality to feel hurt that no one cares enough to ask what she thinks or how she feels. While it is true that those of us who are not naturally sensitive and caring like the Perfect personality need to learn to be more sensitive, the Perfect person also needs to take responsibility for entering into the conversation. The Perfect personalities must be willing to express themselves to others so their real personality can be known and appreciated.

Think Positively

The term *perfect* is ascribed to the Perfect personality because these individuals desire perfection from themselves and expect it from others. This natural tendency allows them to see all the flaws in people, programs, and plans. I remember when my Perfect personality brother was little, he and my mother were looking at the garden. She was praising the beauty of her flowers when he responded, "Yes, but look at that big weed." If you are a Perfect personality, you need to work on thinking positively. It does not come naturally. Memorize Ephesians 4:29, "Let no corrupt communication proceed out of your mouth but that which is good to the use of edifying that it may minister grace unto the hearers."

Work on offering praise and encouragement to others rather than criticism. Make an effort to watch for opportunities to build up others. Many Perfect personalities feel that endorsing substandard behavior in others will give a signal that it's OK for them to be sloppy in their work or that a particular behavior is acceptable when actually a change should be made. If you are a Perfect personality, you must realize that people are more likely to change or improve with positive reinforcement than with criticism. My Perfect personality husband, Chuck, has learned the value of frequent accolades. He likes those fancy breakfasts I cook for him, and he never criticizes my cooking. Even on the less good days he goes out of his way to thank me. If I am still sitting at the table as he gets up to go to work, he comes to me, leans over, kisses me, rubs my back and says over and over, "good Rabbit, good Rabbit." (Rabbit is my nickname from childhood.) If I finish first and am already doing the dishes, Chuck comes to me at the sink and thanks me. His adulation encourages me to keep making him breakfast every day.

The Powerful Personality

Since the ultimate goal for Powerful personalities is production and accomplishment, their communication style tends to be brief and to the point. They often bark out commands to others with little thought for feelings. While this approach is practical and keeps distractions to a minimum, the Powerful personality has to work on improving her overall communication style, too.

Be Interested in Others
Because of the Powerful personality's basic bent toward production, people often get in the way. Additionally, the brusque manner of many Powerful personalities makes others afraid to even approach them. All of us who share the Powerful personality type need to make an effort to improve our communication by being genuinely interested in others.

This can be done in several ways. One way is to listen to others complete sentences and their full stories. The Powerful personality is a quick thinker and she often knows what the other person is trying to say long before the complete thought is finished. Therefore, Powerful personalities have a tendency to cut off other people's sentences and terminate their stories. These people are always looking for the bottom line. In a fast-paced manufacturing plant, this style of communication may be effective between boss and employee, but that would be the only place! In general the "get to the point" approach of the Powerful personality shuts people down and limits future communication.

I remember several years ago when my sister and her husband were buying their first house, she and my mother went house hunting. They looked at many strange and unacceptable houses. My Popular, Powerful mother wanted to share the story with my Powerful, Perfect father. As she went into detailed descriptions of each house, my father's patience wore thin. He interrupted her and simply asked, "Did they buy a house?" To which she replied, "No, but ..." He cut her off by saying, "I do not need to hear about all the houses they did not buy." With her balloon burst, my mother discontinued her conversation about the houses. This abrupt type of communication has the potential to close the door to *any* communication, frivolous or functional. Even if you have already heard the entire story before, being interested in what others have to say encourages open communication.

Lighten Up
The old cliché about stopping to smell the roses is good advice to all Powerful personalities. Because we are so work-focused, we don't take the time we should to invest in ourselves and others. In our communication style, this is played out in a single focus approach. Whatever is important to us takes up all of our time and energy. Therefore we have limited ability to

converse on topics of interest to others.

A friend once told me how disappointed she was that, as an adult, she now had several areas of shared interests with her father, but his focus on his work had become so consuming that unless she wished to discuss his work, there was little else about which they could talk. He had been a tennis pro in his younger years. She had been taking tennis lessons, yet he showed no interest in joining her on the court, or even in sharing tips with her. Over the years their communication has dwindled to perfunctory telephone calls and birthday cards. Due to the single focus of his Powerful personality, neither truly has any idea what is going on in the other's life.

As Powerful personalities, we need to lighten up and broaden our areas of interest. This might mean watching a bit more TV, especially the news shows (who would think you ever have to suggest that someone watch *more* TV?), taking up a sport, or spending more time outdoors—anything that will expose us to something different. As we broaden our horizons, we will find that we have more interests and are more approachable.

Ask Rather Than Demand

Remember the magic words—"Please" and "Thank you"—you were taught as a child? In the bottom-line communication style of the Powerful, these niceties are frequently ignored. Without the word *please* before a request, it becomes a command, removing the feeling of option and building resentment.

In teaching about the personalities, I sometimes divide the audience into small groups. Then I ask the participants of each group to list what they especially appreciate about each personality type and what they wish they could change. The most common wish for change in the Powerful personality is that they would *ask* rather than *demand*.

My friend Lisa told me about a Powerful personality acquaintance. Lisa was offended that this person, whom she hardly knew, had sent her some information and asked her to deal with it by a specified date, only a couple weeks away. The Powerful personality had not developed a relationship with Lisa. They had just worked on a project together. This person had not called ahead and asked if Lisa had time for a new project; she just sent it on because she had a need to have it finished quickly.

When communicating with others, those of us who have Powerful personalities need to remember the "magic words" and be especially careful of our tone of voice. I am always surprised when words I thought I have said in a lovely and gracious tone are received as if they were a harsh barb. Our true personality comes through more than we realize. A good verse for the Powerful personality to memorize is Proverbs 16:24: "Kind words are like honey—enjoyable and healthful" (LB).

The Peaceful Personality

While the Peaceful personality and the Powerful personality are opposites, they do have something in common: neither is very expressive. The Powerful communicates in a brief, sometimes rude, manner. The Peaceful is hesitant to communicate at all, especially with those who are not well known. They are very likable people, content and lacking in any obvious flaws in most aspects of life. Yet, despite their lack of faults, these people have areas in which they, too, can improve their communication style.

Get Enthused

One of the easiest ways for the Peaceful personality to improve communication style is to get excited about something, almost anything. For them it may feel phony. The Peaceful personality is by nature too low key and measures all of life in terms of energy expenditure. Frankly, as my Peaceful grandmother used to say, there isn't much worth getting all "geehawed up" about. However, this is the very thing this personality needs to do—get all "geehawed up." When someone does something you like or gives you a gift, work to be expressive. Be effusive! Muster up all the superlatives you can think of. A lack of enthusiasm will cut communication short and other people will eventually discontinue their interaction with you because they feel discouraged by your lack of interest.

I used to write promotional copy for as many as two new books a week. I would interview the author, scan the book and look for the current news angle or emotional hook to make radio stations want to feature an interview with the author. In our office a young college student worked as a part-time assistant. Melissa was a Peaceful personality and we all loved her. Since she was currently enrolled in English classes, I would ask her to proofread my work. She would review it and put it on my desk with lots of red marks. I frequently found myself following her and asking her if she liked my copy. "Did it make you want to read the book?" I'd ask. Melissa understood personalities. After a few times of my running after her, she started writing enthusiastic comments on the paper in addition to the needed corrections. Occasionally, she even waxed eloquent over the wonderful job I had done. As a Peaceful personality she had learned to get enthused! If you are a Peaceful, remember Philippians 4:8 tells us to look for the praiseworthy things!

Express Opinions
Where the Powerful personality needs to learn to tone down an opinionated nature, the opposite personality, the Peaceful, needs to learn to express her opinions. When asked what she would like to do, where she would like to go, whether she would like coffee or tea, her standard answer is "I don't care," "it doesn't matter," or "whichever is easiest."

Many of my friends have the Peaceful personality and I have learned that in most cases, they truly do not care. However, most people give up asking and just do what they want to do after attempting to communicate with the Peaceful personality and repeatedly receiving the "whatever" response. While at first this may seem like a suitable solution, it is a short-term fix that creates long-term problems.

My husband is a marriage counselor. Many times he has told me of cases where the Peaceful spouse has felt worthless, insignificant, and unimportant in the marriage. The other spouse, usually a Powerful personality, long ago took over the decision making in the home, leaving the Peaceful personality to simply take orders and follow in the wake. While it may have been a relief in the early years to not have to decide, a decade or two of being treated as an invisible person often leaves the Peaceful personality feeling worthless.

If you are a Peaceful personality, protect yourself and generate respect from others. Learn to voice your opinion. Maybe not on every issue. Maybe you really do not care about coffee or tea. But there are many areas that you probably really *do* care about—where you live, what you eat, where you go for vacations. Start by expressing opinions about the things that do matter to you. By doing so, you will gain the respect of others and open lines of communication.

Open Up
Popular personalities spew out more details about their lives than anyone wants to know. They need to learn when to be quiet. On the other extreme, Peaceful personalities need to open up, to share what they are thinking and feeling. Peacefuls are proud of their stoic tendencies, but it is those very cool traits that shut down avenues of communication, making the Peaceful personality seem indifferent and apathetic. Pay special attention to the conversation tips offered in the chapter three. Work on sharing your ideas and projecting your voice.

Remember, communicating effectively isn't just talking, sharing ideas, or speaking to others. Communication is a two-way street. We need first to know our natural traits so we can capitalize on our strengths and work to overcome our weaknesses. As we work to minimize the distracting communication habits that are a part of our personality type, communication becomes more effective.

two

Communicating to
Other Personalities
∾
MARITA

One of the best ways to improve your communication is to adjust your natural communication style when speaking with others who have a different communication style. In chapter one, we reviewed some of the ways we can easily and quickly identify others' personality types. As you understand more about other personality types, you can adjust the way you approach other people. You can succeed by giving others what they need.

At a recent seminar, one saleswoman shared that having a grasp of this information netted her a large sale that she believed she would not have gotten otherwise. She is a combination of the Powerful and Popular personalities, which meant she is an especially strong person who could be intense at best and obnoxious in the extreme. She had an appointment with a Perfect personality. Knowing that Perfects are systematically scheduled and task oriented and that they are low-key people, she modified her behavior accordingly. To make sure she would be on time, she arrived early as a courtesy to his busy schedule. When the gentleman was ready to see her, she entered his office in a much more subdued manner than her own normal behavior. She shook his hand and got right down to business.

All the facts and figures were handy. Without an understanding of personalities, she probably would have been late—although she most likely would have had a very entertaining explanation. She might have told him numerous stories about her product and why he should buy it, but she would have risked making him feel that she was wasting his valuable time. Her respect for this man's schedule and her professional approach worked, met his needs, and won her the business.

Romans 12:18 tells us that the only people we are responsible for are ourselves. The only actions and reactions we have to be concerned about are our own. We cannot change other people, but we can change the way we approach them.

Most of us feel an immediate kinship with those who share our communication style. We connect with them instantly, but we struggle with others who do not share our communication style. Let's look at some simple things we can do when communicating with people of differing personality types.

The Popular Personality

Since the Popular personality is a natural talker, our tips for communicating with others focus on modifying or limiting all her chatter.

When speaking to a Powerful personality, the Popular person needs to stick to the bottom line. When a Powerful personality understands that you are not just rambling aimlessly, but that your comments are purposeful and to the point, he or she perks up and listens.

If you are married to a Powerful personality, you may have

to work at undoing the patterns that years of tuning you out have set in place, but don't give up. If you cut out the extra details in your speech and stick to the point, the Powerful personality will pay more attention, thereby enhancing communication. Picture the Powerful personality as the conductor of the orchestra. Never play unless the baton is pointed toward you and then only play the notes as directed. No spontaneous solos! Remember what Proverbs 15:2 says: "The tongue of the wise uses knowledge rightly, but the mouth of fools pours forth foolishness" (NKJV).

When talking to a Perfect personality, the Popular person needs to be sensitive to the schedule and level of interest of that person. One day while I was doing a radio program on this topic, a Popular personality woman called in to talk about a communication problem she was having with her Perfect personality business partner. She explained that she worked in sales and was out in the "field" all day, while her partner did the bookkeeping and computer work. It worked well for them. One day she had a particularly great sale and was very excited about it. She could hardly wait to share the good news with her partner. She thought that, since her sale benefited both of them, he would be enthusiastic. But what happened was that when she bounded into his office and loudly proclaimed her success, instead of being excited for her, he gave her one of those "if looks could kill" kind of looks. When she called in to the radio program, she was confused.

I am sure that if you are a Perfect personality, you know exactly what the problem was. But if you are like this woman and are a Popular, you too are probably questioning what was wrong.

I explained to her that the Perfect personality is a task-focused person who runs life on a schedule. When she barged into her partner's office unannounced, she disturbed his train of thought and intruded on whatever he was doing. Even though the news was good, it was not received well because of the timing.

The better approach, the adjusted plan, would be to knock on his door, even if it were open, then in her best FM deejay voice say, "Excuse me. I have some good news to tell you. When would be a good time?" To which he might reply "Now is fine," or "In fifteen minutes; just let me finish this up." Then I told her to go to her office, close the door, and call a girlfriend with whom she could go into full and energetic detail about the sale. She'll have time to share it later at the appropriate time with her partner. Ecclesiastes 3:1 puts it just right: "There is a time for everything, and a season for every activity under heaven" (NIV). This basically describes life's process for the Perfect personality, that there is a place for everything and everything should be in its place—and that includes spouses, business partners, and friends. Respect their time and space.

When you are communicating with a Perfect personality, schedule into the conversation any lengthy or important things you need to discuss. Be careful not to barge in or interrupt in the midst of other activities or conversations.

When communicating with the Peaceful personality, the Popular can utilize her natural ability to be positive and encouraging. Make an effort to look for the good in the Peaceful. One day, at a seminar I had been teaching on this subject, I addressed the concept of giving the Peaceful personality a sense of value. A Popular/Powerful woman approached me and assertively asked, "How can I give her a sense of value when she doesn't do anything?" Therein lies the basic problem. The Peaceful personality needs to be encouraged for who she is, not just for what you think she should be. Certainly, offer encouragement and praise about what she does, but be sure that you lift the person up for who she is as well. Some of the ways you can do this are through through cards, notes, or e-mail. (Much more about that later.) Let her know how much you appreciate her.

As Popular personalities, our gift for looking at life through an optimistic filter can be an encouragement to others, especially to the Peaceful personality. It is the little things we do for others and say to them that mean so much and build a lasting foundation of respect with a Peaceful. "Therefore encourage one another and build each other up, just as in fact you are doing" (1 Thessalonians 5:11, NIV).

The Powerful Personality

One of the great strengths of a Powerful personality is the ability to think and act quickly. However, this very asset is one of the things that hinders her communications. A Powerful personality needs to slow down to improve communication skills.

When a Powerful personality talks to a Popular personality, she needs to make an effort to be interested in her colorful stories. The Popular personality always seems to have the most interesting things happening in her life. Even if the event was something that does not put her in a very good light, the

Popular loves to tell what has happened to her. Since the Powerful personality has that ever-present "to do" list on her mind, she tends to view the Popular's stories as an interruption. If she stops what she is doing and gives the Popular personality a few minutes of focused attention, actively listening to the story and responding to her traumas, she will usually find it didn't take all that long.

When I was a child, I liked to give my mother a review of the books I had just read. Of course, she had already read the Dr. Seuss books by which I was enraptured. She had things to do, but I wanted to tell her my "story." I trailed her around the house, telling her one part after another. If I did not think she was listening, I would repeat a section of the story. She now says that if she had just stopped and listened to me, it would have taken half the time!

The Powerful needs to be careful not to crush the spirit of the Popular personality. Powerfuls must heed Colossians 4:6a, "Let your speech be always with grace, seasoned with salt."

A friend of mine related the story of how she had tried to "teach" a Popular how to act appropriately in a particular situation. My friend remarked, "Can't you act any way other than childish? You do not need to be the center of attention all the time!" That Popular is no longer among her friends. My friend was just trying to help. She was not aware of the differences between personalities at that time and as a result used poor communication. If you are a Powerful personality, remember that Populars need you to pay attention to their stories.

When a Powerful personality speaks with a Perfect, time is a factor as well. The Perfect is a detail person and has a very complex mind. While you will not have to listen to many of her stories (the Perfect personality is not a storyteller by nature), you do need to allow her time to share her thoughts and ideas. The tendency for the Powerful personality is to listen long enough to get the gist of the topic and then move on—either physically or emotionally. The Powerful personality's "moving on" effectively shuts down communication.

Dodi Osborn is part Perfect and part Peaceful personality. She told me about a principal for whom she worked who was a Powerful personality. He would ask teachers for their ideas and input on policy decisions. After they went to lots of trouble and work researching and thinking through the issues, they became justifiably angry and resentful when, time after time, he tuned them out, ignored their input, and did what he wanted. Powerful personalities should remember Philippians 2:3-4, "Let nothing be done through selfish ambition or conceit, but in lowliness of mind let each esteem others as better than himself. Let each of you look out not only for his own interests, but also for the interests of others" (NKJV).

When you are communicating with a Peaceful personality, time is once again a factor. Because Peacefuls do not speak in rapid-fire commands, and often take longer to process thoughts than other personality types, the Powerful personality is likely to dismiss them and shut them out. In this case, the Powerful needs to work on developing patience and good listening skills. Make an effort to give the Peaceful evidence that her ideas and thoughts are important too. A wife who finishes sentences for her husband is probably a Powerful personality, married to a Peaceful personality man. Resist the urge to speak for another. Respect and time are two important issues for the Peaceful personality.

The Perfect Personality

Listening is a natural skill for the Perfect personality. These people like to process information. However, the Perfect personality will need to work on what she says, how she says it, and to whom she is speaking. The Perfect personality tends to notice flaws and may use a comment about a flaw as a conversation opener. She might say something like, "I noticed that you have a tear in your hem." This may not be too well received.

When you are talking to a Popular personality, this approach is especially problematic. Populars crave praise. If you are a Perfect and you are talking to a Popular personality, look for opportunities to compliment her. Make an effort to praise others, opening conversations with a positive comment, such as, "That dress is a great color for you!"

Also, while the Popular personality is not a joke teller, she is used to having people laugh at her stories. Some of those stories sound foolish to the practical nature of the Perfect personality. You will open lines of communication with the Popular personality if you respond openly to her humor by laughing. At the time of this writing, I have been running the Southern California Women's Retreat for seventeen years. For fourteen of those seventeen years it has been held at the same hotel. Numerous salespeople have taken care of my business. Usually we get along great and I feel as if the person is my good friend. However, one year I did not click with my salesperson. I thought she did not like me. She was efficient and did her job well, but I did not enjoy working with her. I tried to figure out the problem by closely observing our next few interactions. At the time, I was also dealing with the catering manager of the same hotel. When she and I talked, she frequently laughed at some little comment I made or a quip I threw in. Then I realized that my problem with the salesperson was that she did not think I was funny. I do not really think of myself as someone who is funny, but I realized that I was used to others laughing with me as we talked. From that point on, I had most of my communication with the catering manager. I was glad when the salesperson was promoted for her efficiency. I wish all salespeople understood my personality and had a note in their file that says, "Marita is a Popular personality. She needs you to laugh when she says something funny."

Whenever you are communicating with a Powerful personality, remember she has a "to do" list. Most Powerfuls want to accomplish more in a day than is humanly possible. While you may have done lots of research on a topic and have unlimited knowledge, Powerful personalities are not the ones with whom to share it. Just give them the bottom line, the essentials. If they ask questions, answer them with a "sound bite." Take a breath and allow the Powerful time to jump in. If they do not jump in, take over or move on, then offer supporting details. Let the Powerful know that you have additional information if she would like it. Above all, do not answer questions she did not ask.

At the Christian Booksellers' convention, the booth next to ours was selling Bible software. The Popular personality salesman, Rick, kept talking to me, encouraging me to come try some. When I finally consented, Rick was not available, but his Perfect personality partner was. I was very interested in their product, so I asked for a demo. Boy, did I get one! All I wanted to know was how the thing worked and did I need to read a manual to use it. I wanted to put my hands on it and try it. This Perfect personality man (probably the one who developed it) went on and on about how this software would allow me to commune with God. He walked me through all kinds of features, while internally I was tapping my foot, eager to get my fingers on the keyboard and play. It never happened.

Fortunately, they gave me the basic program to sample at the end of the show. I took it home and installed it on my computer and I love it. I am using it in the writing of this book. I did not need to read any instructions or watch a video. The Perfect's sales job told me far more than I wanted to know or had time to listen to!

When you, as a Perfect personality, are speaking to a Peaceful personality, you really need to watch for positives and freely offer praise. Words cost you nothing; you can give them away without harm. "Pleasant words are a honeycomb, sweet to the soul and healing to the bones" is the wisdom of Proverbs 16:23.

The Peaceful Personality

Communication does not come naturally for the Peaceful personality. They are natural listeners, but true communication requires both sides, giving and taking. Tips to the Peaceful for improving communication with others all involve advice on what to say and how to say it.

When you are communicating with Popular personalities, remember they are inherently creative people. They have ideas popping out all the time. Some of their ideas you will like, and some you will think are nonsense. When they have an idea you think has merit, get excited about it. This may feel phony at first, but you will see it reap rewards in the communication department, plus it's scriptural! Galatians 4:18a tells us that "... it is good to be zealous in a good thing always." Your excitement might include a vocal exclamation over the idea's value. You could share the idea with others, giving the Popular personality full credit for creating the idea. You could show physical approval by hugging her enthusiastically, since Populars like touch. You can't embarrass them. They like being the center of attention.

When you are talking to a Powerful personality, try to speak more quickly than your usual pace. Practice reading a paragraph and time yourself. Then try it again, aiming to cut 25 percent off your reading time. Then try again, aiming for a 50 percent decrease. You will find that you can probably get the sentences read in half the time. Make a note of that pace and try to use it when talking to Powerful personalities. Give only the basics, the bottom line. Never fall into the trap many of us used when taking a school test composed of essay questions. Sometimes when we did not study properly, we would write until we had enough material to appear to have answered the question. A Powerful personality will ask, "What's your answer?" or "What is your point?" Respond to the Powerful as though you were on a witness stand and the Bible put before you was open to James 5:12: "Let your 'Yes' be yes, and your 'No' no" (NIV).

As a Peaceful personality, Debbie has learned to think through in advance what she wants to tell a Powerful personality. By doing this she can give them succinct information, and be ready to answer any questions. This prevents the Powerful reaction of impatience. She has found this technique to be especially helpful in dealing with her Powerful boss!

Conveying something to the Perfect personality is different. This person is not in a rush. Perfects appreciate facts. When speaking to them, offer them facts and back those facts up with documentation. This is especially important in work situations. Prepare in advance. Think through information and develop research documentation (or at least sources where it can be found) to have on hand for the Perfect personality. This will satisfy his or her need for facts and will help you feel prepared. You may not ever need to share the document you have prepared, but the fact that you have it validates what you are saying.

All of us, regardless of our specific personality, have areas where our communication will be easy, where we are strong. And all of us have areas in which we can improve. As you first identify your own personality and work to improve the specifics mentioned here for your personality type, you can then work on identifying the personality types of others. You will be able to adjust what you say and how you approach others for the most effective communication.

three

Communicating Through Conversation
∾
MARITA

When we think of communication, one of the first things that is apt to come to our mind is conversation. Conversation is one of the most basic forms of communication. Yet, while we converse every day, most of us could do it more effectively. The dictionary defines conversation as "the act or an instance of talking together; ... a verbal exchange of ideas, opinions, etc." However, as women, we know there is much more to a good conversation than just "talking together" or "a verbal exchange of ideas." A good conversation is something that nourishes our souls and satisfies many of our deep inner needs.

Just before I sat down to write this chapter, I had a long telephone conversation with my dear friend Georgia. Yes, we talked together. Yes, we exchanged ideas. But when we hung up, we each felt that far more than mere talk and a simple exchange of ideas had taken place. A good conversation offers stimulation, support, and security.

"The truth is that conversation is an enduring human need in every age."[1] "An enduring human need." It is a need, isn't it? Especially for us women. The bonding and connection we feel after a good long chat helps to carry us through some of the stress and difficulty we face.

49

Hectic schedules and the myriad of responsibilities we face too often make finding time for good conversation difficult. One way I fit conversation into my life is through the use of a cordless headset telephone. I put the headset on, dial the phone number of a friend and drop the keypad into my pocket. I then talk while I cook, do dishes, clean, or fold laundry. It makes the chore go by much faster and allows me to invest chore time into an enduring human need. Whether we find time to chat over the telephone, over a cup of coffee, or during a long drive, we need to find time for conversation.

Since time is so limited for most of us, we need to make those conversations we are able to snatch as meaningful as possible. One of the most important things to remember about conversation is that it is talking *together*, a verbal exchange. It is not one person (usually the Popular or Powerful personality) talking while another person (usually the Perfect or Peaceful personality) listens. That is a monologue. A conversation involves an exchange, a give and take. It may involve two people or several. Regardless of the type of conversation you are involved in, there are things you can do that will make it easier and more effective.

Share the Opportunity to Share

There are talkers and there are listeners in the world. It is easy to let the talkers talk and the listeners listen. However, if you have ever been to a social gathering, such as an extended family holiday dinner, you know that a constant flow of information from one person is boring. The experience leaves you wondering what is going on in the lives of others around the table.

When I was a child my father had rules about conversation. I did not always appreciate his rules because they curtailed my chatter. However, as an adult, I have come to appreciate the foundation his rules have given me. Now I pass them on to you—not as rules, but as concepts worth implementing whenever possible.

Rule 1: We were each allowed only a certain percentage of the conversation. Our family had five members. That meant each of us could have 20 percent of the conversation. My father, of course, was the one who policed each family member's time. My mother and I, who are both the Popular/Powerful combination, always used up our allotment early in the mealtime. My brother, sister, and father would have had no chance to share what was on their minds or what had happened to them during the day if my father had not implemented this rule.

When several people are conversing, watch the amount of time you spend talking. Do not take up an unfair portion of the available time. This is especially important advice for those of us who are in the extrovert half of the personality chart— the Popular or Powerful personalities. We need to be careful that we do not turn the others in attendance into an audience.

It is important to draw the quieter ones into the conversation with open-ended questions. If the social gathering is in your home, and you are the hostess, you have a little more opportunity to steer the conversation. But even when you are not the hostess, you can still watch for the person who has not said much. Ask something to draw them into the conversation. Remember, you will be appreciated by everyone if you do not take over the conversation yourself and if you make an effort to bring everyone into the conversation.

Rule 2: Another of my father's rules that I have found to be very valuable is that only one person talks at a time. When that one talks, everyone listens. If you have ever been to a social event where one person is talking to you on one side and another is talking to you on the other, you know how frustrating this can be. You feel like a Ping-Pong ball going back and forth between two totally different conversations. There are some techniques we can use to watch our own tongues and to gently assist in providing direction.

Women, especially, should strive to practice the one-at-a time rule. Because juggling conversations is necessary when running a household or caring for a husband and family, we think we can always do many activities at once. Even when I use my telephone headset, there are occasions when I have to stop other activities and give undivided focus to my friend's part of the conversation.

We should each be sure to stop talking while someone else is talking. For those of us who are the Popular personality, this is harder than it is for others. It seems as if we have a short distance from our brains to our mouths. If an idea comes to us, we blurt it out without taking the time to think it through, or without noticing if someone else is already talking. We need to wait for a gap in the conversation, before barging in with our thoughts. We can learn to control our tongues, so that we do not create conflicting conversations.

If you are talking with one person, and another starts to talk to you, you can graciously hold up one finger and say to the person who is jumping in, "Just a moment. Will you hold that thought?" or "Let me finish here." When you do this, it is important to get back to the second person once the first conversation is completed. Now, giving the second person your full attention, you can turn to them and say, for example, something like. "I'm sorry. I really want to hear what you have to say."

Ask Interesting Questions

When we look at conversation, it boils down to two simple parts. The first is to ask interesting questions, ones that draw people out. Ask questions that cannot be answered with a simple "yes" or "no," but rather gives the person an opportunity to share what he or she is thinking.

When I was single and dating, I had a question I used with the various gentlemen. I asked them, "In reality, if money were no object, what would be your fantasy vacation?" The "in reality" part eliminated ideas like going to Mars (although that's not so far from reality anymore). The "if money were no object" part allowed their imaginations to run wild. After thinking about this for a moment or two, if he got misty eyed and suggested backpacking in the Rockies, catching fish in the crystal streams, cooking them over an open fire, and sleeping under the twinkling stars, I knew I would not be dating him again. The question allowed me to get to know each man's values—and camping under the stars was not something I valued at the time.

In the article on small talk mentioned earlier, Michael Korda offers a line that he says is guaranteed to produce conversation. He suggests looking at whatever piece of jewelry a woman is wearing and saying, "Tell me the story of how you got that." While this comment is not directly a question, it produces the same result. It draws the other person out and allows you to get to know her. It is something to which you can't say "yes" or "no." Your jewelry, it may be an heirloom piece, a gift from a friend, or an inexpensive item you picked up to go with a specific outfit. Chances are you have a story about it.

Korda's line is a great way to start a conversation with a total stranger almost anywhere. You could use it at your husband's high school reunion when you feel out of place. You could use it at a reception where others seems to know everyone. Remember, events like that are full of people who feel equally alone. Watch for someone alone and use a good opening line to begin a conversation. You just might make a lifelong friend!

If you feel awkward or inexperienced at asking questions, there are several books that can help you. One I recommend is simply called *The Book of Questions*. Written by Gregory Stock and published by Workman Press, it has over two hundred different, interesting questions. All of the questions require more than a "yes" or "no" answer and may all help you get to know another person better. It is not written from a Christian perspective, so you may want to pass over some of the questions. I am sure that you will find several questions in it that feel right to you, questions you would be comfortable asking. Jot down those questions and tuck the list into your wallet or organizer. Next time you are with someone new or feel at a loss, sneak a peak at the questions you have selected and ask away! After you do this for a while, you will find that you become comfortable asking your own original questions, without the help of printed text.

Mom's Canned Questions is a "can full" of conversation starters designed to be used at the table. Since this product has a Christian emphasis, no checking or editing is needed! The company has now produced several editions, including one for Christmas and one for teachers. *Mom's Canned Questions* is available at most Christian bookstores (Mom's Family Preserves, 1-800-771-MOMS).

Be Eternally Fascinated

Asking interesting questions is a great place to start a conversation. However, for questions to become conversation, there is another important part that must be included—listening!

If you are a Popular personality, you are prone to engage in idle chatter. If you are a Powerful personality, you think others are prone to engage in idle chatter. For both personalities, attentive listening is a challenge.

A friend of mine enjoys traveling. She and her husband will use any available reason or excuse to travel to most anyplace. She is the Powerful and he is the Popular personality. Everyone has a backup personality style; fortunately for their marriage, they both have a good share of Popular personality. His secondary style is Peaceful. Their first few trips caused challenges in their marriage, beginning with their honeymoon. Both are challenged by the need to listen. Guess what happened when they asked for directions? Neither one really listened and then they blamed each other when they got lost. My friend, the Powerful personality, received directions about turns or signs by saying "OK" while someone was trying to make sure she understood. Her husband's efforts were equally incomplete. His requests for directions always included telling the person he was asking where they were from, why they were there, how cheap the rental car was, how many children they had, and on and on. He would never admit he did not give the person talking enough time to give adequate directions. By the time the two of them bought a map, sat on the side of the road, and figured out how to get to the hotel, they were barely speaking to each other.

After nearly twenty-five years of marriage, they have finally mastered the art of getting directions. She now carries a small notepad and writes down all the directions as they are given. She repeats them to be sure she has correctly heard what the person is saying. Only after the directions are complete will she allow herself to engage in small talk. If her husband is asking for directions, he still starts his conversation by telling the person facts they probably could have lived a lifetime without. However, now the last of the conversation consists of getting the directions accurately. He may even ask the person to write them down for him. Populars are so charming that everyone loves to help them; sometimes he even gets a free map. He smiles, thanks them, and grins all the way to the car. They laugh now about their early experiences in traveling, and pat themselves on the back for conquering the challenge of directions. They have learned that both of their personalities make them inattentive listeners.

Recently I heard a talk by Pat Harrison, the cochair of the Republican National Committee. She said that she was from New York and that for New Yorkers there were two parts to conversation, "talking and waiting to talk."

We can improve our listening skills by practicing listening. Communication expert Paul R. Timm suggests that one helpful listening exercise is to focus intently on something that it does not matter whether you listen to or not—something like the first ten minutes of the nightly news. Pretend that you will be required to give a detailed report the next day. Force yourself to make copious mental notes.[2]

Executive Female had an article on small talk. I love the advice they offered on listening: "Focus on the other person. Be an excellent listener, an active listener. Be eternally fascinated."[3] Victoria Chorbajian coaches people in speaking and presentation skills. She says eye contact gives the impression that you are listening, "The second your eyes move away, it conveys that you're losing interest."[4] Active listening means summarizing what you think you just heard. Encourage active listening skills, says sales training consultant Linda Pogue. "Don't wait for the end. If it turns out that you haven't heard right, you won't have time to fix it. At each turn of the conversation, add such comments as, 'Now, as I understand it, these are your top three concerns.'"[5]

I remember the first time I met Christian singer Jillian Ryan. We had talked on the telephone and had a great time, we hit it off right away. Our mutual business had us on the phone together frequently. We finally decided we should meet face-to-face. We lived an hour or so apart so we met at a restaurant halfway between. We spent two hours over lunch and talked so much we barely came up for air. Years later I remember what fun that meeting was.

As we were getting acquainted, Jillian would ask me a question. As I answered, she was not just quiet. She was an active listener, she was "eternally fascinated." While I was answering her question, she leaned on her elbows on the table, looked me in the eyes, and truly listened. She nodded and said things like, "Hmm...." or "And then what happened?" Both her body language and her words told me she was listening. Her additional questions pulled me deeper into the story. She was not just making conversation, she was listening. She was interested. I was amazed at how quickly the time flew by! I assured her that the next time I would ask her the questions while I listened. Before our lives took us in different directions to different states, we did get better acquainted and I did listen.

At 103 and 105 years old, the now deceased Delany sisters wrote their second book, called *The Delany Sisters' Book of Everyday Wisdom.* In it they offered all kinds of advice gathered in their over two hundred collective years of living. Their advice included: "Learn to listen. There are a whole lot more big talkers in the world than there are big listeners. Know when to keep quiet. When we have something that's private, we call it 'graveyard talk.' That means it is a secret. That means it is between you, me, and the tombstone, honey."[6]

Being Likable

Good communication skills are essential for both personal and professional growth. A survey on qualities employers prefer in employees lists good speaking skills, good writing ability, and good interpersonal skills at the top of the skills list. Appearance and education were at the bottom of the list. [7]

In his book *You Are the Message,* media consultant Roger Ailes talks about Bennett Cerf, former chairman of Random House, Inc. He says, "Bennett always seemed to be in good humor … and he had a tremendous interest in other people. After spending ten minutes with him, you would find yourself engrossed in a deep conversation—usually about yourself. More than anything Bennett had the quality of being likable.

In my work as a communications consultant and media advisor, I've discovered that if people like you, they'll forgive just about anything you do wrong. If they don't like you, you can hit everything right on target and it doesn't matter."[8] When we ask interesting questions that draw people out and we listen actively, being eternally fascinated, we are not only communicating effectively, we are also gaining the added bonus of being likable.

James 1:19 gives us good advice on conversation by saying, "Be quick to hear, slow to speak, and slow to anger" (NAS). When I speak on this topic, I call this section "consent" or "consideration." Consent simply means to agree or to give approval. I find that in many conversations we find ourselves not agreeing with the speaker. Sometimes the things we disagree about are major issues, worthy of debate. But more often than not, the issues on which we disagree and over which we become angry, are not worthy of disagreement. This is where consent comes in.

When you are engaged in a conversation with someone and a topic comes up where differing opinions exist, ask yourself, "Is this worth ruining the relationship over?" Most of the things we argue about are silly things, surely not worth the destruction of a relationship.

Job 6:24-25 says, "Teach me and I will be silent; and show me how I have erred. How painful are honest words! But what does your argument prove?" (NAS). What does our argument prove? In many cases there are two or more correct answers or approaches to a situation. An adage says there are three ways to do something, "my way, your way, and the right way." "The right way" usually means a compromise, and we can choose this more likable way, offering agreement or consent, even if it is not the way we would do it. Romans 12:18 tells us that, "If possible, so far as it depends on you, be at peace with all men" (NAS). While we cannot control the responses of other people, we can control what we say and how we react.

In the words of eighteenth-century essayist Joseph Addison, "Good nature is more agreeable in conversation than wit, and gives a certain air to the countenance which is more amiable than beauty."

Part Two

❧

Communication Complexities

four

They Just Don't Get It!

∾

FLORENCE

When I talk with women who have marriage problems, they always say, "We don't communicate." We all know how to talk, but to have an equal and noncombative conversation seems close to impossible. We women understand each other, but somehow our men don't seem to "get it."

When any potential social pitfall is mentioned, we women run it through our minds quickly and get intuitive feelings about how each person involved in the scenario will react. We instinctively know that Melissa will feel left out, Mother will drop into a depression, Susie will scream, and we will be left trying to pick up the pieces. Our mates are bewildered. "How did you figure that all out so quickly?" they ask in amazement. Some add, "That's ridiculous!"

Yet when you get together at Susie's for Sunday dinner, Melissa feels left out because she has to sit at the card table with the children, Mother is depressed because she wasn't invited until the last minute, and when the men begin to argue over politics, Susie screams. You're left to break up the fights, cheer up Mother, and make Melissa feel part of the crowd. You're also left with the dishes as Susie has gone sobbing to her room and the others quickly leave. They just don't get it.

What Makes Women Different

Are you involved with people who just don't get it? Do you wonder why, when you drop hints big enough to wrap up and sell, that your man doesn't get it? Do you have children that have been told one hundred times not to stand on a particular corner, yet when you catch them there, they reply, wide-eyed, "Oh, I didn't know you meant *that* corner!"? Why do we get it and they don't?

One reason is that we have a sixth sense, intuition, that tunes into relationship problems. For the most part, women's intuitive powers are not understood by men. Often during our marriage my husband, Fred, made business deals I didn't feel right about. He would have charts and statistics to prove his point, and I had nothing to offer but my feelings. In the long run, though, my feelings were usually better than his facts. As I have listened to thousands of women's problems over the years, I have realized many times over the worth of a woman's intuition and have suggested to men that, if their wife has a creepy feeling about a potential employee, they shouldn't hire him or her.

I remember a suave gentleman who came to our business office for an interview wearing a velvet jacket and a silk ascot. He was extremely complimentary to me, and Fred was impressed with his sophisticated manner. When I mentioned that I wouldn't trust him, Fred was stunned and asked me why I would jump to such a hasty conclusion. "The ascot, for one thing," I replied. Fred thought my comment to be a potential crusade against ascots and hired him to be our sales manager anyway. Within six months he had propositioned me and embezzled thousands of dollars. Now if I say, "I don't feel right about this," he answers, "That's good enough for me!"

We women can make feeling judgments, and yet how seldom men believe we can be right without a shred of evidence or a chart and a pointer. Maureen went to a chiropractor who was charming and attentive to her every ache and pain. When her treatment was over he patted her on the rear and told her he'd need to see her again the following week. She made the appointment but became increasingly concerned over going back. With no more facts than a little pat, Maureen called and canceled the appointment. Within a few months Maureen spotted an article in the local paper. This same doctor had been arrested for sexually abusing his female patients. Maureen was relieved that she had trusted her intuition and wasn't one of his victims.

Susan was getting her training to become a masseuse. One of her required courses was hypnotherapy. At the first meeting the teacher said they could all bring someone the following week to work on. She brought her beautiful teenage daughter and a friend of hers who was a model.

The instructor "helped" many of the women a little too much from Susan's perspective, and he was especially attentive to the two young girls. As the group was practicing relaxation techniques Susan looked over to where the instructor was himself relaxing and noticed that he was intently perusing a Victoria's Secret catalog. This struck her as odd that a man would be looking at pictures of women in their undies while in charge of a class, but she didn't say anything about it.

At the end of the session the instructor announced a special drawing for two private sessions of hypnosis with him. Everyone got excited as he drew names from a hat and, would you believe it, the two young girls won the prizes. A full hour alone with the teacher!

The more Susan thought about the situation, the more concerned she got. She shared her fears with her daughter, who accepted her mother's opinion. The girls didn't go to the free appointment. Who knows what might have happened, but by not going they prevented the possibility.

Gayle moved back into her hometown and needed a babysitter. Her Uncle Ted was available and free, and her family insisted that she use him. Her mother explained, "Your uncle is a lonely man with nothing to do and he loves little Rebecca. It would be stupid to pay money to some unknown person when you have a blood relative available at no cost."

With such a convincing argument from her mother, Gayle gave in, even though in her heart she knew better. Each time she took Rebecca to the good uncle's house, she felt worse. Soon the little girl fussed at going and clung to Gayle's skirt. One day when Gayle stopped by to pick up Rebecca the child ran to her in terror.

"What's happened to her?" Gayle asked. As Rebecca sobbed, good old Uncle Ted confessed that he had touched this child inappropriately, along with some other nieces he had cared for. When Gayle came to me for help she was justifiably furious at her uncle, but she was equally upset with herself for being shamed into a situation she knew was wrong. "If only I'd trusted my instincts!" she cried.

Tina, my longtime friend, could certainly understand Gayle's anguish. A devout Christian who had taught marriage classes in her church for many years, Tina had seemed to have a picture-perfect Christian family. She and her husband had reared two quiet, polite sons whose intelligence and high grades earned them full college scholarships. One was studying to be a doctor; the other had hopes of becoming a missionary.

Imagine my surprise when Tina called me during a recent holiday to say the past year had been the worst of her life. Her two sons were in deep trouble, she said. The medical student had become a drug addict, and the would-be missionary had dropped out of college, announcing he no longer believed in God.

When we discussed possible causes for these calamities, she told me her husband had so tightly controlled the boys as they were growing up that they had a seething rebellion inside that burst forth when they got away at college. She admitted that she had known what her husband was doing wasn't right, but each time she tried to voice an opinion he would counter her firmly with the same three reasons: "You are only a woman and don't understand male things; you had no father so you have no sense of male bonding; and you have had so little education that you couldn't be trusted to make valid judgments. Leave the raising of the boys to me." This set of statements had wiped out any alternate opinions. Tina had gone through years of teaching on submission and thought she was the prime example of the perfectly submissive wife by meekly accepting her husband's dominance.

There's no guarantee that her sons would have turned out differently if she had been able to voice some objections, but as she looks back she says, "Why didn't I trust my instincts? I knew better and I did nothing about it in the guise of sweet submission." God gave us women intuition. Let's not throw away the gift!

When We Don't Communicate

Besides intuition, the other reason women "get it" and men don't is that we sometimes can sense unspoken feelings that men can't hear. Unfortunately, this can also cause trouble when we "hear" the *wrong* feelings. This ability also makes women assume men know what we're thinking when in fact they don't have a clue. We talk all around our feelings without presenting facts clearly; we belabor inconsequential details and set our mates' minds adrift. We ask for the verdict, but they don't even know they're on the jury.

This is reinforced to me every week as I listen to women who are in deep marital problems. When I ask why they didn't do something before their marriage got to a crisis point, they all reply, "Well, I told him we needed help, but he didn't seem to get it." If this kind of miscommunication is a consistent problem, what can we do about it? Are we just mumbling our way through the marriage maze? Have we never made our case clear?

In spite of my God-given ability to communicate, I realize I've been guilty of halfway hints and fuzzy phrases. Early in my marriage, because of my "Father Knows Best" indoctrination, I didn't think I had the right to point out Fred's mistakes. If he said he'd take us all on an outing next Saturday and on Saturday he forgot and left for the office, I'd moan and groan a bit as he went out the door. I'd tell the children, "You can't ever count on men; business comes first." They learned to never get excited over Dad's promises of trips and outings until they were actually in the car. When Fred would come home after a Saturday in the office, I'd be a little distant to express my disappointment, but now that I look back on it, I know he didn't get it.

He interpreted my behavior as lack of appreciation for how hard he worked to support us. I never sat down with him and asked him realistically how many Saturdays a month he could give to the family. If we'd settled on even one, we could have made some plans; I could have pointed out how important it was for him to be trusted to keep his word; I could have mentioned the children's anticipation several times in a positive way and probably he would have followed through. Instead I'd hold him accountable and not remind him, then wait for him to announce he was going to the office. My glares and groans made him glad he had chosen the office over a day with the children and me.

If it's true that men don't get it as easily as women, is there something we could do to help them along? Think of the last situation where you ended up frustrated over a misunderstanding. Had you made your point perfectly clear or had you approached the subject through the back door?

When Gloria got her first view of her husband's new secretary, she was upset. Entering her husband's reception area, she came upon a young woman in a skintight miniskirt leaning over a file drawer. But it was even worse when this new employee turned around. She had on a thin T-shirt and seemed to use her ample breasts to gesture as other people would use their hands. All the men in the office were focused on this creature, and Gloria was furious. She got even more upset when she found out the girl's name was Trixie. *It fits her perfectly*, thought Gloria. *This will never do!* That night Gloria created a "don't-get-it dilemma" at home.

"I think it's important that women dress modestly in office situations, don't you?" she asked her husband, Jim, during a commercial break of "Monday Night Football."

Jim, who is not into hypothetical discussions at nine in the evening, answered, "I guess so." (He didn't get it.)

"What do you mean you guess so?" Gloria retorted angrily. Jim looked up, stunned that Gloria could possibly be upset over a generic problem that had nothing to do with them personally. Now she got somewhat to the point. "How could you have hired someone named Trixie?"

The focus now was on the new girl's name, and, because it came across as an attack on Jim's judgment, he was forced to defend himself. "I think it's an acceptable name. What do you want me to do, ask her to change it?"

"No," Gloria now tried the sulk approach. *If I look down and appear depressed, he'll have to ask me what I'm really upset about.* But he didn't. Instead he asked himself if Gloria could be losing her mind. As he pondered this possibility, Trixie came to his mind. He focused on how she had looked that day, then glanced over at Gloria, who was huddled up on the couch, pouting.

As he was mentally playing with the comparison, Gloria tried a new approach, "Did you see how that Trixie looked when she bent over the file drawer?" He hadn't noticed, but the idea was not an unpleasant one. "Why are you smiling? Have you been watching her all day?"

Another attack, totally missing the original point, caused more defensiveness. "I have a lot better things to do than stare at Trixie all day. What is your problem, woman?"

"Her skirt is too short."

"If you had legs like hers you could wear short skirts."

"See, you did notice! Are you in some kind of midlife crisis or something?"

"I was just sitting here minding my own business, and all of a sudden you decide I'm in a midlife crisis!"

Jim didn't get it. And it's not really his fault. Men want the bottom line, and they don't easily pick up hints or back-door approaches. How could Gloria bring up the problem clearly without an attack? What was she really trying to accomplish? Was Trixie's name a valid issue? Wasn't it her choice of clothing that was the problem? Let's consider another way Gloria could have presented her concerns:

"Jim, I was so glad I dropped by the office and met your new secretary, Trixie," she could have said. "She seems like a pleasant person and she surely has a great figure. I did notice when she bent over that I could see her underwear and when she turned around I saw that her T-shirt was too revealing. I think for your own reputation among your clients, you had better have her dress more conservatively. It took you a long time to build this business and you wouldn't want anyone to get the wrong idea."

In this direct approach to the problem, there is no attack. The problem is made clear, and Gloria puts herself on Jim's side. The result? Jim gets it.

Here's another example. Marg has just found out that the Johnsons are going to Hawaii for the third time. She and Morris have never been and she wants to go. She begins her approach at dinner.

"The Johnsons are going to Hawaii again."

"That's nice." (He doesn't get it.)

Silence reigns.

"Is that all you have to say?"

"About what?"

"About the Johnsons going to Hawaii!?"

"I didn't know you had asked for my opinion."

"I didn't. I just told you they're going and it's their third trip. I want to go."

"Did they ask you?"

Marg is now beside herself. "No, they didn't ask me!"

"Then why are you so mad?"

"Because I want *us* to go. I want you to take me. We never do anything exciting anymore."

"Are you trying to say we should take a trip to Hawaii?"

"Yes!"

"Then why didn't you say so?"

"Well, I tried."

But not very well.

We women need to realize that our back-door approach doesn't often work. We are dealing with men who don't get it. Some of them work hard at not getting it; others just come by it naturally. When past methods haven't brought positive results, our increasing frustration has turned some of us into screaming shrews and some of us into silent statues.

Does it really matter that we are not communicating effectively on things that are not life threatening? Isn't it easier to talk about subjects that aren't controversial? Many couples only talk about superficial topics: the children's grades in school, what restaurant to go to, who will rule Cuba once Castro is gone.

What Fred and I have learned is that when we shut down discussions on emotional topics and became pleasantly agreeable in order to stay happy, neither one of us really knows what the other is thinking. For example, when I just went along with things without showing interest or asking questions, Fred entered into business ventures without telling me the risks involved. We both recognize that I have a sixth sense about hiring people, but since I wasn't involved in the interviewing I had no input into the hiring decisions. Because I had let minor things slide with no meaningful discussion, Fred saw no reason to involve me in major business decisions. It took some extreme losses to make us see that we were both wrong. I could easily have put all the blame on him (it seemed so obvious, at least to me!) but then I realized I was at fault, too. By setting a precedent and not making my feelings known—not making sure he got it—I had given him silent permission to hide anything that might be bad news.

Our changes did not come overnight, but as Fred could see his pattern of shielding me and I became willing to discuss matters instead of pulling back, we began to climb up the hill to meaningful communication.

Dropping hints and beating around the bush lead to frustration. Hot tantrums and cold shoulders block reception. Whether it's your husband, your child, or your friends who haven't heard the truth, help them.

They'll get it.

five

Be of Good Cheer:
Compliments and Criticism
∽
FLORENCE

For those of us who wish to be effective communicators, whether one-on-one or on a platform, we need to make a commitment to the Lord that we will put the needs of our listeners before our own and that we will share graciously rather than preach or put other people down. In this chapter we will look at our attitudes as we aim to be a blessing to others. We will see the value in having a cheerful disposition, in giving genuine compliments, in receiving compliments graciously, and in handling criticism without reacting defensively.

In Scripture we are admonished to rejoice, to be full of joy, uplifting, thinking on positive things. The psalmist proclaims, "This is the day which the Lord has made; we will rejoice and be glad in it" (Psalm 118:24, LB). Peter tells us, "Rejoice with joy unspeakable and full of glory" (1 Peter 1:8, NAS). Paul, who wrote of joy in adverse circumstances, proclaimed, "Rejoice in the Lord always: again I will say, rejoice" (Philippians 4:4, NAS).

If we believe in the consistency of biblical direction, we would all be looking for the best in others, giving out words of encouragement, presenting Silver Boxes to all we meet. Wouldn't it be exciting if we had the assurance that everyone we were to meet tomorrow would give us compliments? Would it help if we gave out compliments to others even if we got nothing in return? Can giving to others make us feel better about ourselves?

Because my husband and I fly so frequently, we are often upgraded to first class. It is a small section and the flight attendants can spend more time with customers. Fred and I always smile and acknowledge each attendant when we board. We don't complain and we compliment them on their pleasant nature in a stressful situation. We find out about their families and, as we inquire, they often show us pictures of their precious children. Toward the end of the flight at least one will come up and thank us for being so nice to them. We ask, "Isn't everyone nice to you?" They groan and tell us horror stories about what has been said to them. We feel we have behaved normally, but they see us as bright lights in a difficult day.

Articles are written about how rude people are to each other and how manners and civility are things of the past. But does that mean we should give up and say, "What's the use?" Are these thoughtless people all out there in the world or do we also run into them in our Christian activities? I was asked to speak at a breakfast meeting of a large Christian organization. Fred and I were led to a table near the stage, where all the seats were filled except our two. The lady who brought us introduced us to the others and left. Our names, if the people heard them, meant nothing and they went on with their conversations, ignoring us completely. One Powerful personality woman was holding court and giving words of wisdom to everyone within reach of her voice. The people on each side of us were facing her and no one spoke to us during the entire meal. Fred got up and poured coffee for everyone and they seemed to accept him as the waiter. When the chair of the event arrived on the platform, she introduced me and I went up to speak. When I had finished, I returned to my seat, at which point the controlling woman looked across the table and asked me, "Why didn't you tell us you were somebody? We would have talked to you."

What do you say to such a person? Do you give her a lecture on snobbery? Do you lose your own joy and snap back at her? Just because others are rude doesn't free us to say what we please. I looked at her, smiled, and said, "I'm sorry; I didn't think of it." She was happy with that answer and we parted friends.

For those who wish to communicate on a positive level, we need to "rejoice always, again I say rejoice." We need to repay bad with good and not fall into the negative traps gaping before us. The world desperately needs cheerful people who will smile and spread joy wherever they go. Are you that kind of person? Do you get up each day and look forward to blessing others? Do you make it a habit to speak kindly to others? Many people you meet today will be downcast and sick at heart. Proverbs 17:22 says, "A merry heart doeth good like a medicine." Why not look at yourself as a traveling doctor giving out merry medicine. Wouldn't that be fun!

Give Compliments

Not only should our attitude be cheerful, but our words should be encouraging. Practice giving an uplifting word to everyone you meet. Find something sincere to say to make their day a little brighter. Their looks of surprise and gratitude will be your reward. Tell your husband you are so glad to be married to him. Send him off with a warm word he can remember in the trials of a difficult day. Say good-bye to each child with a compliment, such as, "You look adorable today," "I know you'll do well on your test," or "Thank you for being so cheerful; you brighten up my day." Express to your friend that she is very important to you. Let your manager know how much you appreciate his or her leadership skills.

Many of us mothers feel that our children understand us, that what we say in anger or sarcasm will not bother them. We think they will say in their sweet little minds, "Mother's having a bad day. She didn't mean it when she said I was stupid. She meant to be funny." Is that the truth? Or do they internalize the words without processing the stress that produced them. As I counsel with adult women who have a low sense of worth, I ask them what it is they don't like about themselves. They tell me they are homely, ugly, cursed with limp hair, fat, no good, stupid, clumsy. Then I ask, "When did you first feel that way?" With little hesitation they respond, "My mother always said I was ugly"; "My father told me I was too fat and no man would ever love me"; or "My brothers said I was stupid."

In many cases these repeated comments were intended as motivation. People assume that if you know that no man will love you fat, you'll stop eating junk food, but unfortunately the reverse is true. Children accept our negative comments as fact and don't turn our words into motivation. Think for a moment about something someone said to you when you were a child. I remember the woman who looked at my two little brothers and said to my mother, "Aren't they adorable!" She then looked at my awkward ten-year-old self with the Dutch-cut bangs and said, "She must be smart." I remember thinking, "I'm obviously not adorable. I guess I'd better get smart."

Why do we remember these comments? Because they hurt us and we accepted them as truth. What does this tell us as parents? That we had better change our habit of lashing out at our children and weigh our words. Every negative becomes a burden that our children carry with them to their deaths. Do we want to be responsible for their low self-worth as adults? Certainly not! Make your family your top recipients of positive words.

Some of us as speakers live two lives: the face we wear at home and the one we use outside. However, if we use unguarded words at home, some are bound to slip out in public. The pastor in *The Scarlet Letter* had kept a secret from the whole town. He never owned up to the fact that he was the father of Hester's baby. He allowed her to be punished by wearing the scarlet *A* for adultery while he was free. Toward the end of the book, he has some moments of regret and introspection and says, "No man, for any considerable period, can wear one face to himself and another to the multitude without finally getting bewildered as to which may be the true."

We don't want to be confused leaders. We want to be consistent. If we rejoice in each day and give positive words at home, we will be true to ourselves and others in public. Philippians 4:8 is a convicting verse for me: "Whatsoever things are honest, whatsoever things are just, whatsoever things are pure, whatsoever things are lovely, whatsoever things are of good report; if there be any virtue, and if there be any praise, think on these things."

Why not make a list of these attributes and then check off which ones your husband has, then each child, then your friend or manager? Is there any virtue in any of them? Is there any quality worthy of praise? If there is, focus on these good points and thank them for their strengths. God's Word doesn't say to wait until these other people are perfect. It says if there is any virtue, just a little tiny dot, or anything worthy of praise, then find this, be grateful for it, build on it for the future. Don't tear it down and destroy the hope for the future. When we practice giving out kind words at home or in the workplace, we will have no problem being gracious to the people in other aspects of our life.

Often, as I go from place to place, I meet women who feel led to tell me about the previous speaker. Seldom do they share about the ones they liked, but instead about those whose walk didn't match their talk, those who wouldn't go near the people but hid away backstage, those who wouldn't eat with the committee but insisted on room service, those who got angry because their name was misspelled on the program, those who had a temper tantrum when they missed the plane. You can't be gracious with the people around you when you are selfish and angry inside. What you are really feeling tends to come out, even when you do not think it shows.

As you work to give out compliments to everyone you encounter, be sure that the compliments you offer are truly uplifting. When Marita speaks on this subject, she advises people to watch out for what she calls "counter-compliments." Like counterclockwise, a counter-compliment is one that is intended as a positive word but somehow leaves the recipient feeling worse than before. As you work on giving out compliments, run them through in your mind before letting the words out of your mouth. Rather than saying, "I like your hair much better today," which leaves the person wondering "What was wrong with it yesterday?" you could simply say, "I love your hairstyle!"

Marita practically grew up in the public eye. She began speaking with me when she was around thirteen years old and began speaking professionally on her own when she was nineteen. Many times she will speak at an event where someone in the audience heard her speak ten or twenty years ago. They come up to her with enthusiasm gushing out all over and say, "You are so much better than you were the last time I heard you!" While Marita knows they mean well, it is hard not to wonder, "Was I that bad before?" The better way to offer words that are "like honey—enjoyable and healthful" (Proverbs 16:24, LB) would be to say something such as "I really enjoyed your presentation today."

When you give compliments, affirm one another, lift each other up. The words to Barb and Toby Waldowski's song "Affirm One Another" are a good reminder:

When we affirm one another
You can feel the love begin.
A glow lights the countenance
and the energy flows in.
I cannot think of a kindness
that is so powerful, so fast.
Only a word fitly spoken does the task.

Receive Compliments

Some Christian women feel that it is a sign of humility to deny any positive words given to them.

"You did so well as hostess of the luncheon."
"It was the Lord. I really had nothing to do with it."

"I love your ring. It sparkles so brightly."
"It's really nothing. Just something my husband gave me."

"You always wear such beautiful clothes."
"I try, but I never think I look right."

When we develop a habit of negating positive comments, people cease to give them. If your husband says your hair looks pretty, don't answer, "It didn't come out right at all." The next time he likes the way you look, he won't tell you for fear of being rebuffed. To be the gracious women we want to become, we must be grateful for every positive comment we can gather in. All we need to say is, "Thank you." If we wish to add a story about where we got the dress, who made the drapes, or who does our hair, this will amplify the praise. We must be careful not to make comments that will make the person complimenting us feel stupid.

Many years ago, before I ever had been on the *Focus on the Family* radio show, women would occasionally tell me how much they had enjoyed me on Dr. James Dobson's show. I would say, in truth, "I've never been on that program." Some got angry at me: "Well, I heard you!" Some wanted to argue. The response was always negative. Now, no matter what program people think I was on, I just say, "Thank you. I'm glad you enjoyed it." They go away happy.

Listen to what you say in response to compliments, remembering to bless the giver of glad tidings. And if you get credit you don't deserve, it will make up for what you didn't get that you did deserve.

Accept Criticism

No one likes to be put down or criticized, but the more public we become the more people feel free to place judgment upon us. What should we do about accepting criticism? What I wrote on this subject in my book *It Takes So Little to Be Above Average* helped so many people that I am quoting the material here.

"Not one of us loves to hear what's wrong with us; no normal person looks to be hurt. We all wish our friends and family loved us unconditionally, as they should, but we are all realistic enough to know that many people feel led to give us some 'constructive criticism.' Proverbs 12:16 says, 'A fool is quick-tempered; a wise man stays cool when insulted' (LB). Ignoring an insult is easier said than done. How can we learn to handle harsh words?

"Since I always teach from my own experiences, let me share how I developed a plan for accepting the worst. As I analyzed my dislike for negative evaluations, I determined I would learn to 'take it.' I would grit my teeth and accept whatever was dumped on me. This 'keep your mouth shut' attitude kept me out of trouble, but it didn't calm my turbulent insides. The more active I became in the speaking world, the more criticism I received. I became a believer of James' statement, 'Let not many of you become teachers ... for you know that we who teach shall be judged with greater strictness' (James 3:1, RSV). I decided 'taking it' wasn't enough; I had to take it cheerfully. As I prayed about the ability to do this, the Lord showed me I had to *be thankful* for each comment. You mean—say 'thank you' for criticism?

"Let's think about this possibility. What does the person who gives you unsolicited advice expect from you? He expects you will become defensive, lose your Christian cool, and therefore validate his opinion that you have a problem and aren't practicing what you preach. Since you don't want to give him this affirmation of his evaluation, accept his advice cheerfully and thank him for it. This stops him in his tracks in a most positive way and prevents him from proceeding to points B, C, and D.

"In pursuing this plan, I have developed some helpful answers where I don't have to resort to lying. I may not think much of the idea, but I can always say, 'Thank you for sharing that thought with me'; 'Thank you for the time you put into this analysis'; 'Thank you for caring enough to point that out'; 'I appreciate your thoughts, and I will surely discuss them with the staff'; or 'I must say, I have never considered that before, but I will give your suggestion some thought.'

"All of these comments are positive and true and will deal with the critic cheerfully. As you become good at accepting criticism and develop your own style of response, you can then move on to the third step: Ask for it. That step is the graduate work in our Christian living. We feel we've made progress when we can first take it, then take it cheerfully. But when the Lord is really in control of our lives, he will prompt us to ask for advice. So often in Proverbs it says that a wise man asks for counsel, while a fool despises instruction, and that if you rebuke a wise man he will love you, but a fool will hate you. If a wise man loves rebuke and I want to be wise, I must look for helpful suggestions. I must ask for evaluation. How could I have done even better?

"As I perceived this plan as a path to wisdom, my defensive attitude disappeared and I developed a spiritual willingness to seek counsel. I don't want to be one of Solomon's fools. Indeed, 'Better is a poor and a wise child than an old and foolish king, who will no more be admonished' (Ecclesiastes 4:13).

"Former Chief Justice Charles Evans Hughes once said, 'If you can accept and profit by criticism, you have a priceless ability possessed by few of your fellow men.'

"So ask yourself three questions: 1) Are you willing to take criticism? 2) Are you willing to take it cheerfully? 3) Are you willing to ask for it?

"Let's assume you wish to be wise and not foolish. What should you do when you receive a critical comment, admonishing advice, or a scathing scenario? First, you should swallow hard and take it. Then you should smile, if possible, and instead of defending yourself, thank the person for caring enough to share these thoughts with you. Let him know you will take these ideas to heart and give them consideration. If you're ready for graduate work, ask for some further help or suggestions.

"Now that you've passed your finals, what should you do with this new information? You should run it through the 'fact filter' in your mind: If it's wise, true, and applicable, act upon it. If it's foolish, false, and ridiculous, forget it. How do you know the difference? Ask the Lord to guide you. If when you test 'Am I sarcastic?' some clear examples come to your mind, you should accept this possibility and work prayerfully to overcome your tendency to make humor at others' expense. If someone says, 'You'd look a lot better if you would smile once in a while,' ask a close friend if you need to smile more. If she hesitates in answering, you'll know this is a problem you need to work on.

"What if you sift it through the 'fact filter' and it makes no sense at all? You should say, 'Lord, if this thought is as foolish as it appears to be, help me to forget it.' 'A wise man's heart discerneth both time and judgment' (Ecclesiastes 8:5b).

"After speaking at a retreat for three thousand women in Michigan, I received a large envelope containing the audience evaluations of my performance. I read each one and found the majority to be extremely positive. Several mentioned that the second half of a skit I had produced was too long. I listened to that tape with this thought in mind and agreed it was too long. I profited from these comments and improved the product.

"One lady wrote, 'Florence was unexpectedly exciting, which goes to show appearances are deceiving.' When I ran this through my mind, I came up confused. I was glad I was exciting, but I wasn't sure what had been deceptive about my appearance. I'll never know, but I surely shouldn't waste much time brooding over this evaluation.

"Let's learn to accept suggestions and even insults cheerfully. Let's ask for evaluations and listen thankfully. Let's run them through our mental 'fact filter.' If they're valid, let's act upon them. If they're of no consequence, let's forget them.

"Patsy Clairmont is an exceptional communicator and gifted humorist. When she was first on our CLASS staff, she was weak and in poor health. We were all concerned about her, and it fell upon me to make some suggestions. Her initial reaction was defensive, as is natural, but the next evening when I went to my hotel room there was a note on my pillow. 'Thank you for caring enough about my health to make suggestions.' Through these suggestions she was put on a positive program which has led her up the long road to improved physical strength and stamina. She is now an energetic and dynamic speaker and the author of several best-selling books.

"When we accept and profit from what we didn't want to

hear, we do have a priceless ability possessed by few. Today practice smiling when less-than-positive statements are made about you."[1]

My sister-in-law Nance has a precious statement she makes when someone gives her a negative or critical comment. She smiles and with her soft Texas accent she says, "Thank you. I'm sure there's a compliment in there somewhere."

Look for the best. It just might be there.

six

Effective Written Communication:
The Paper Trail

∾

MARITA

In a society where everyone has a telephone, and most people have several, written communication is almost a lost art. Picking up the phone is quick and easy, but there are many times when written communication is preferred.

One of those occasions might be when you are extending an *invitation* to someone. You can call, but a written invitation provides the recipient with a written reference of all the pertinent information. *Thank-you notes,* which have become a lost art, are often better than phone calls, because the recipient can read and re-read your kind words. Frequently, electronic mail *(e-mail)* or a facsimile *(fax)* is the best way to communicate, and both of these miracles of modern technology are written forms of communication.

Invitations

An invitation for an event such as a wedding is easy because there are books full of sample wedding invitations to follow. The less formal events trouble us most. We tend to either phone an invitation or resort to the "store-bought" form invitations, making it easy to simply fill in the blanks.

Many of us have not been taught some of the common cour-
tesies that provided a framework in previous generations. Our
invitations need to include more than just the time and place.
Many people do not know that "RSVP" requests a reply from
them. It is our job to include all the information we possibly
can to assist our guests.

One time I planned to have a dinner party for my husband
and all of his colleagues and their spouses. I printed an invitation on my computer. It was a cute and funny invitation. I
delivered them to the office. Everyone responded except for
one family. Finally, on the day of the party I called them to be
sure they were coming. They were not planning on attending,
but had not told me. I had bought food and set the table
including them. They did end up coming and brought their
children, whom I had not counted on. We set a place in the
kitchen for the kids but the entire event was a frustrating one. I
have had other occasions when I thought I invited only adults
and the entire family came, causing me to quickly reset the table
and serve smaller portions to everyone.

Mishaps like these have made me realize that an invitation
must be extra informative. When planning any kind of invitation, start with the journalistic *W*s: Who, Where, What, When,
and Why.

The "Who" is who you are inviting and will usually be
included on the front of the envelope. It can also be "Who" else
you are inviting, which might be the office team, or the entire
neighborhood. As a part of the "Who," indicate whether this is
an adults- or couples-only event, or if the invitation is for the
whole family.

The "Where" is where the event will be held, probably at
your home. But it could be at a restaurant, in a park, at a base-

ball game, or in any number of locations.

The "What" will indicate what type of event the invitation is for. Is it a meal or just dessert and coffee?

The "When" is important so people know when to show up, and should include both the date and the time.

The "Why" indicates why you are having a gathering. It might be a birthday party, an open house, or a housewarming. It could be a barbecue or a formal dinner party. Perhaps you are celebrating an anniversary.

While your words will indicate "what" the event is for, the style of the invitation will enhance the message and help the recipient know if the event is formal or casual. This was my error in the invitation to my husband's colleagues. The event I had planned was a celebration of his anniversary with the company. It was a formal event, with all our good china, crystal, and sterling, an elegant tablecloth and cloth napkins edged in gold, candlelight, and classical music. But because I was just learning computer graphics I did the invitation like a pictograph, using pictures and a childlike font. It was a very cute invitation and I had a great time creating it, but it sent the wrong message that the evening would be very informal.

For a formal event, the invitation should be printed on a paper that has the appearance of an engraved edge, or a parchment scroll, or even marble. All of these finishes would lend an elegant air. The font used for the invitation should not be a childlike one, but instead formal, perhaps with an Old English flavor. For my Labor Day barbecue, I've used a paper with a flag motif and a font with a patriotic look. These types of invitations will also help the guests know what attire is appropriate.

The basic "when" is obviously the time the event begins. However, since most people today lead very full lives, I suggest giving an option. We once were invited to arrive at 3:00 for a cookout. We arrived at 3:00 hungry, only to find that the meal would not be served until 6:00. We ate every cracker and morsel of cheese we could find during the three-hour wait. To be more effective, the "when" should say something like "We'll be serving at 6:00. Please feel free to arrive anytime after 3:00 for appetizers and fellowship." This gives your guests the option to arrive early or late, depending on their own schedule.

If the event is an open house and guests can drop by anytime, be sure to indicate that on the invitation and indicate an ending time. You might say, something like "We are inviting all of our friends over for an open house. We will have light refreshments. Please feel free to drop by anytime between 2:00 and 4:00."

The "why" part of the invitation is especially important when the event traditionally includes gift giving. If you do not wish the guests to bring a gift, be sure to say so. This is also when a written invitation is helpful, so pertinent information can be reviewed.

Chuck and I were invited by phone to a party; we were both sure we were told "no gifts." However, when we got there, everyone seemed to have a gift for the "birthday girl." After the dinner and cake a big production was made of the opening of the gifts. We felt really out of place.

Thank-You Notes

At our CLASSeminar, we talk a lot about outlines, and we will address them more in chapter nine. However, they are very helpful even in basic written communication, like invitations and thank-you notes. The *W*s suggested for invitations—who, where, what, when, and why—are an outline. They provide a skeleton which you simply fill in with information. The same can be done with an effective thank-you note, although the outline will be different.

Barbara Bueler, who spent many years as a part of the CLASS teaching team, created this easy-to-remember outline for sending an effective thank-you note: Personal, Purpose, Plan. The personal part mentions something about the recipient as a person and tells this person that he or she is special. The purpose is the actual thanks and specifically mentions the gift, the good time, or whatever is appropriate. The plan indicates some future contact or repayment of the act. An act of kindness makes us want to do something for the other person.

The following example thank-you note includes all three parts of an effective thank-you note. As you read it, notice how each part is woven in. It does not say, "Some personal comments are...." "The purpose of this note is to thank you for...." "Now let's plan to get together...." Yet, all three areas are covered, creating a gracious and effective note.

Dear Lauren,

You always know just what to get for a present. When I saw your gift at the shower last week, I knew from the tasteful wrapping paper and the cluster of violets on the top that I would love what was inside.

When I opened the box and saw the white porcelain bunny with those big eyes and pink ears, I was delighted. How thoughtful of you to choose something I can add to my rabbit collection. Thank you for caring and coming to the shower.

As soon as Dick and I are settled, we'll have you and Randy over for dinner.

With love and appreciation,
Judy

A thank-you note is appropriate any time anyone has given you a gift, especially if it was sent by mail and the giver is not present to see you open it. Avoid sending a preprinted note that simply says, "Thank you for the gift," unless you personalize it as well. If you were invited for a meal, or someone did something nice for you, write a note! In *The Family Book of Manners*, author Hermine Hartley says, "For any gesture of kindness shown to us—a visit, a gift, or anything that made us feel good—we should try to send a thank-you note as soon as possible."[1]

An additional nice touch is to send a thank-you note when you have had guests in your home. Once I had the opportunity to go to the home of Bob and Emilie Barnes for a meal. Emilie's home is warm and lovely. She is an excellent cook and a gracious hostess. I left thinking I must send her a thank-you note.

However, the next day brought its own set of crises and the thank-you note did not get written. I was still thinking about it when I received a note of thanks from Emilie! While I do not recall the exact wording of the note, I know it made me feel so special and went something like, "Thank you for coming to our home last night for dinner. It was great to see you and Chuck again and we enjoyed catching up on your lives. We'll have to do it again soon!"

I was so touched by Emilie's thoughtfulness, I decided that I wanted to do the same for my guests. Unfortunately, I am not quite as organized as Emilie. While I intended to send my guests a note the next day, it didn't happen. Nor did it happen in the days or weeks that followed. Before long it was too late to bother with it.

Then I stumbled onto this plan, which I have shared with

thousands of people in my seminars and which has been used successfully by many.

I like to take pictures. I almost always have a pack of recently developed prints with me that chronicle my recent escapades. When I have guests over and I have done an especially nice job of setting the table, I like to take a picture of it before the guests come. Once everyone is there, seated, and having a good time, I get the camera out again. Using what I call a Ph.D. camera— ("Push here, Dummy"), I simply tell everyone to look my way, push the button, and know that I have captured the moment and the memory. Sometimes that shot was the last on the roll and I have the picture the next day. Other times it may be weeks or months before I finish that roll and get it developed. When I get the photos back, or when I organize them into an album, which may be months later, I send a copy of the print to the guests with a note. The fact that I am sending the picture seems to excuse the tardiness, as everyone knows that it may take months to use up the roll. I send a note with the print that starts out with: "I just got my pictures developed" or, "I have finally had time to get my pictures organized and into the photo album." Then I continue:

"When I saw this picture of our dinner together, it made me smile. What a great time we had that night. Your presence made it so special. You really know how to keep the conversation lively! I hope looking at this picture brings back the wonderful memories of that night for you, as it did for me. We must do it again soon!"

"Always give thanks for everything" (Ephesians 5:20a, LB).

Caring

Another time when written communication is the most effective form of communication is when someone is having a difficult time and you want to let them know that you care. In cases like this, the old-fashioned pen and paper method of communication is usually the best. A local computer magazine, *Computer Scene,* offered the following advice: "Please don't use e-mail to deliver condolences to employees who have experienced the death of a family member or friend, or who have suffered some other personal tragedy. A written note is much more appropriate and more meaningful to the person."[2]

My sister, Lauren Briggs, has done a lot of counseling with those who are going through loss. She offers great advice as to what to say to show you care in her book *What You Can Say When You Don't Know What to Say.* Because the book is no longer in print, I'll share her advice with you.

When someone is facing a loss of any type and you do not know what to say, Lauren suggests sending a card or note as the best way to acknowledge a person's pain and to initiate comfort. Additionally it gives you the opportunity to think through what you want to say. Finding the right card isn't easy, however. Johnny Cash was asked why his music is so different from most other country western singers. He replied, "You can tell most of them have never walked in the woods." Greeting cards designed to offer comfort are often like that, offering an empty greeting without showing understanding. They suggest that the person will find peace in the future without addressing the pain today.

Lauren says, "I found a card that clearly addresses the fact that many disturbing events happen in people's life for which we have no explanation. It says, 'It must be hard to understand.... I don't understand either, but I love you.' When someone dies in an accident, is diagnosed as having a complex disorder, has lost a job for no apparent reason, or is going through some other Job-like loss this is a good one to send.

"Another card emphasizes God's unconditional love and acceptance, 'He comes to us where we live.... He loves us where we are.' As friends we need to express love and communicate the fact that no matter what situation they are experiencing, we (and God) accept them where they are and stand with them. Other cards are more general, but still offer appropriate support. One says, 'You are in my thoughts and heart.' Another, 'I'm praying for you today ... and tomorrow too!' Knowing you are thinking and praying will uplift your hurting person and bring her comfort in an otherwise sad or lonely day.

"Many have told me that they felt their friends wanted them to be strong and not cry in their time of grief. A card I send frequently very delicately allows for tears. 'To let you know I care and wish I could soothe the empty place inside your heart where the tears are born.' This expresses your concern and inability to take the hurt or fill the empty place, but also lets the bereaved know that tears are a very natural response to that empty place.

"These cards are not the only ones to send, but they are an example of the kind which express the appropriate emotions to your hurting friends. Before you can really minister to their needs, you must acknowledge their hurt, and tell them in your card or note that you care, support them, share their anguish, are praying for them, and love them unconditionally.

"The card you send is very important and will serve as a demonstration of your love and support. The person to whom you send it will probably read and re-read it many times for years to come. While its printed message will minister, so will the personal note you add.

"When my grandmother passed away, I received many touching cards. One friend wrote, 'I have always admired you for the caring and patience you have shown in taking care of your grandmother. I am sure that being a part of your home enriched her life.' It was special to know that my friend saw the effort it took to have Grammy with us, but also knew the special relationship we had.

"Another friend wrote, 'Having lost my grandma, I can relate to the loss you are feeling. No one can take the place of a dear grandma!' If you have shared a similar experience with the person you are writing, tell them in your note. Another thought is to include what the individual meant to you. One mother in our church wrote, 'Grammy was always cheerful and interested in my baby Jacob. I will remember her fondly. Grammas are such precious gifts. (I still miss mine after fourteen years.)'

"When sending a sympathy card, add a note about what the surviving relative meant to the deceased. My grandmother's sister wrote me a letter shortly after Grammy's death and said, 'Thanks for being such a caring granddaughter to her. She said so many times you were the one person who seemed to care what happened to her. Needless to say there were many others, but you had the knack of letting her know your feelings.' That comment from my great-aunt made all my efforts on Grammy's behalf worthwhile. What a blessing a few sentences can be to an aching heart.

"If you are writing to people you do not know well, be sure to identify yourself and tell them how you knew their loved one. Share a special quality that you admired about the deceased, an impact that person made on your life, or an interesting experience you shared. Remember to address the card to the whole family. Many of the cards I received after Grammy's death were addressed solely to me, even though my husband and children loved her as well."

After a death is an obvious time to send a note showing that we care. However, there are many other types of loss people face that need a note of caring as well. In her book, Lauren included the following chart. When someone I know has experienced a loss and I do not know what to say, I have found this chart to be very helpful. The suggested comments could be made in person or in a written note.

What You Can Say ...

The following suggestions are not word-for-word statements to make, but rather a reflection of a heart-attitude you should have for the hurting person. May God fill you with his tenderness and compassion, enabling you to be an extension of his love.

When you are faced with having to communicate your feelings but you do not know what to say, these suggestions will help you effectively communicate that you care.

Lauren says, "Sending cards, notes, or letters is a good way to make initial contact with someone enduring a crisis. But it is important to remember that the comforting shouldn't stop there. Keep sending little notes or cards to brighten their day. Let them know how often you are thinking of them—what you are asking God to do for them. Send cards that you would like to receive if you were in a similar situation. Many people have sent me cards I've appreciated, expressing their

	DO SAY	DON'T SAY
At a funeral	I'll always remember … I'll come by with dinner tonight.	He's so much better off in heaven. If there's anything I can do, call.
A baby died	I know how much being a mother means to you.	You can always have another one. Be thankful you have Jenny. At least you never got to know it.
Divorce	The future must seem frightening. I'll stay close. I'm sure this is a lonely time for you—let's have lunch.	I never liked the way he treated you. There are two sides to every story.
Legal crisis	It is not important to know what happened. I just want you to know that I care.	Will you lose everything? Tell me how it happened.
Handicapped child	She has beautiful eyes. She is so loving and precious.	What are you going to do with her? If you'd taken better care of her this wouldn't have happened.
Elderly parent	I know how much you love her; I'm sure you are doing the right thing.	How could you put your own mother in such a place?
Loss of home	I've been part of some very beautiful memories here.	Remember our home is really in heaven.
Friend moving	I've seen what special friends you are. I know you'll miss each other.	Well, you can always write.

	DO SAY	DON'T SAY
Pet dies	I know she was important to your family.	It's only a dog!
	Sometimes this brings back other sad feelings.	You can always buy a new kitten.
During terminal illness	How are you feeling about what you are facing?	I know a lady who had the same thing....
	I'll take you to your next doctor's appointment.	Won't you be glad to be with the Lord?
After death of terminally ill	Even though he needed a lot of your time, I know you'll miss his company.	It must be such a relief now that it is over.
Death of a spouse	I know how much he meant to you, and how you'll miss him.	You were so lucky to have him for thirty years.
Loss of body part	I'm sure this will take a lot of adjustment. I'll be with you every step of the way.	At least you still have your mind.
		Be glad it wasn't worse.

love and support. That has encouraged me to use similar ideas to comfort others."

Any time you need to communicate something to someone that they will need to refer back to either for information, affirmation, or comfort, the written word is best. And in these cases, the written word on something tangible like a card or note is the most effective way to communicate.

seven

Written Communication:
Digital Devices

∾

MARITA

W hen we needed to send something quickly, we used to call FedEx. For a fee, they could assure us that our documents would arrived where they needed to be the next day. It was not all that long ago that overnight mail was the standard in quick communications. But that was before facsimiles and electronic mail came into our lives.

Faxes

I remember when the facsimile, now commonly referred to as the fax, first came out—before e-mail. We did not yet have a fax machine at our office, but the Christian radio station next door did. Many of the radio stations we were working with asked us to fax them information. We'd go next door and beg to use their fax. Then we got our own. It used thermal paper and each incoming page needed to be cut. Once the pages were separated, they curled and were nearly impossible to stack without the weight of books on top of them. My, how times have changed.

I now have a nice plain-paper fax at the office and the old

thermal-paper one at home—not to mention a fax program in each computer. We often get calls in our office from people who need information right away, so we offer to fax it. Usually this is great. Within minutes, they have what they need.

Occasionally a caller does not have a fax machine but they really want the information right away. We suggest that she look in the phone book and find the closest copy shop or office supply store. Most of these places offer commercial fax service. Anyone can have a fax sent there. There is a charge for this service, but when you need something right away, the fees are worth it and are usually still less than an overnight charge.

The fax is used for the typical business needs of sending proposals, price quotes, invoices, and lists. However, it is handy for personal needs as well. Karen Hansen shared the following fax story with me.

"I often found that life with a two-year-old left my husband and me with less than enough time to discuss necessary subjects. When it came time to discuss having a second child, we never seemed to reach any decisions while we were talking. My husband finally told me that he would give me his own side of the decision (meaning more discussion would be needed!) in 'two weeks' (his self-imposed time limit). When two weeks came and went without a word on the subject (and I was feeling the biological clock ticking on a daily basis), I decided that I would have to approach the subject in another way that would get his attention, and hopefully lead to a discussion or decision.

"I wrote a direct, heartfelt letter that explained my feelings about it, and I faxed it to him at work. Being self-employed together, I knew this was discreet because he received all of the faxes personally, and I sent it on a day that I knew wasn't going to be particularly busy or stressful for him.

"He called me within a short while, and lovingly said we would definitely talk that evening, and that he hadn't really understood just how important this was to me until he had read that fax. We did have our thoughtful discussion that night, and communicated quite a lot better than we had before! As I write this, I am seven months pregnant with that second child. So I can say from my own personal experience that a fax can be a great method of effective communication, when used appropriately."

Sending a fax has become almost as personal as custom stationery. Edie Veenstra is an artist in Michigan. She has a home-based business doing beautiful custom calligraphy for weddings and greeting cards. She says, "I have a cover sheet that is very decorative. It is a border with flowers at the upper left and lower right hand corner. The styling says (I hope), 'Hey, here is a message from someone who is really an interesting, updated, daring (translated exciting), unusual, artsy, stylish woman.' It is just enough of something to perk up the interest to read the communication, but not too much to overwhelm. It is a half-sheet of paper, too. I really cannot stand waiting for my machine to work its way through a lot of empty space—wastes time and money, I think. This design works well for my calligraphy business and my speaking.

"My husband uses a picture of himself on his fax cover sheets. He has cover sheets with the picture of his secretary for her transmissions. This is really a more personal touch and brings a very positive response from the customers and companies he deals with. You do not feel like you are talking to a stranger and it is also a powerful tool for recognition when he goes to meetings or meets a client.

"I also have a friend who 'collects' funny cards. You know the ones where there is a cartoonish character—usually a woman who finds herself in a predicament and then says something understatedly hilarious about it. You know you are getting a fax from Debi and you need to pay attention."

If, like Edie, you have a home-based business, you might want to consider Jeanne Gormick's advice. She says, "To avoid junk faxes, I never include my fax number on my business cards. Anyone who needs to know the number can be given it on an as-needed basis. This is especially important to our family, because I run a home-based business. It helps to avoid those late-night (automatically computer-generated) faxes that wake us up thinking one of the kids is in trouble. I also call anyone who has sent a late night fax to remind them that I have a home-based business. I did this with our local Chamber of Commerce. I wanted their information, but not late at night. They were most accommodating and even changed their faxing policies once they were reminded that many of their members were home-based."

When my business was in my home, I kept the ringer on the fax turned down as low as it would go. I then closed the door to my office, which was right next to the master bedroom. If the fax rang during the night, I did not hear it.

Whether you are sending a fax for business or personal reasons, you should use a cover sheet. It may be plain or fancy, as long as it represents you, as Edie's is indicative of her style. The cover sheet should include your name, phone number, date, and number of pages being transmitted. Since a fax is electronic, bad connections happen frequently. There are a variety of reasons why a complete fax message does not get through. A complete cover page helps the recipient know if she received everything and gives her the information needed to call and advise you if it needs to be re-sent. Occasionally, we receive a fax that is not intended for us. If the phone number is on the cover page, we call the sender and let them know that their fax was sent to the wrong number. Keeping in mind that faxes can get into the wrong hands, it is wise not to fax confidential material.

In addition to the cover page, Joanne Slead suggests labeling the top of each page of a multiple-page fax with the recipient's name, the sender's name, the date, and the page number. This is especially important for those people receiving faxes on thermal paper (which curls up and gets into amazing messes), or in offices that receive numerous faxes.

The cover page can be used not only for information, but it can also be used as a marketing tool. Deb Haggerty suggests ending your fax with a "signature" such as:

Jane Smith, MBA
1-000-1234 "Speak With Confidence!"
Call for more information.

Additionally, your fax should have a real signature. Signing the fax makes it more compelling and personal. Along that same line, handwriting the cover is apt to get a quicker response because it stands out more. However, be careful that spelling and punctuation are not so casual that your fax appears careless. Remember also that pencil and blue ink do not always transmit clearly.

Once you have faxed a document, I suggest that you stamp it with a rubber stamp that says, "FAXED." Sometimes it is hard to remember if I have actually faxed it, or only intended to.

After the fax has been sent, you may want to mail the hard copy or file the correspondence so you know the history of the transaction or in case the recipient calls and says he or she did not get the fax. Keeping a copy will allow you to re-send it easily.

E-Mail

The fax makes it easy for us to almost instantaneously send an existing document, or one that requires a signature. However, for a memo or a quick note, electronic mail may be the better way to go.

I have a new friend who calls me "techno wizzo woman." I earned this title because I recently helped her create a "homepage." While I do know more than she does, I know far less than many others. I know just enough to be dangerous. Nearly everything I know I learned from my true "techno wizzo" friend Deb Haggerty. She got bitten by the technology bug early on and she knows everything! So, when Deb told me about on-line services and e-mail, I listened. I tried it out and I, too, was hooked.

I love e-mail! It is a great way to stay in touch and communicate informally, yet effectively. It has the amazing ability to help you stay in touch with people you would not contact otherwise. Yet it allows a comfortable distance so that you can stay in communication when a relationship is strained. Electronic mail can pull both extremes into the center.

Paula Johnson says, "I definitely keep in much closer contact with my friends and relatives who have e-mail, and I encourage people to get e-mail if they want to feel close to any of their 'people' who are quite a distance from them! I feel closer to, and know more about, one of my younger sisters and her family right now than I have in the past thirty years, because she got e-mail about five months ago! What a blessing!"

Bonnie Skinner is a friend of mine. As a grandmother, she felt ill-equipped to jump into the electronic world of communications. However, she did get a new computer that had a modem and allowed her to utilize e-mail. Now she uses e-mail to stay in touch with her family. She says, "Our oldest grandson, John, is a freshman at Texas A&M and is a member of the Corps of Cadets. This is a stressful time for him. Since we cannot talk by phone, I can send him an e-mail daily as an encouragement—so that's what I do. Our phone bill has decreased by about 60 percent since I have been on-line."

Bonnie also uses e-mail for her various enterprises. "In this business of writing and speaking, it is not only convenient but great fun to share comics, comments, contributions, and other such things with our comrades via the electronic systems. My first order of business each morning is to answer the e-mail. That, in itself, sets some priorities for the day—like a staff meeting would do. Via e-mail I conduct business and coordinate conferences, meetings, etc. Because of the time factor, in using e-mail one quickly learns to make quick, clearer decisions without elaborate discussions. We cut to the chase and get to the point. As coordinator of an upcoming women's conference here in San Antonio, I have been afforded the luxury of literally planning the entire conference without direct communication with the other participants. E-mail and faxes do the work for us."

E-mail allows you to think through your comments or response before they are sent to the other person—unlike a phone call or a face-to-face conversation. Similar to a verbal conversation, you get a quick turnaround or response. However, like written correspondence, you can review what you have written. E-mail gives you the best of both worlds. Since e-mail is a more informal mode of communication, you can depart firrom the strict structure of a formal memo or letter. Speaker and author Kathy Collard Miller says, "As a Perfect, I've had a difficult time not writing a 'tome' or book every time I respond by e-mail. The neat thing about e-mail is that you don't have to be long. I'm learning to be brief! And it's OK. It isn't rude!" In a note you mail in the conventional method, you would never write just two sentences. It would be a waste of paper and the page would look blank. You might pick up the phone just to ask a question or share a thought, but what if the other person is not in or it is after hours in the other time zone? You might forget what you wanted to say by morning. These are cases where e-mail shines.

One of my favorite benefits of e-mail is that I can write something one time and, with the touch of a button, it goes to all my friends! Most e-mail programs, either through the Internet or a commercial service such as America Online, Microsoft Network, or Prodigy, have address books built in. Within these address books you can individually list the e-mail addresses of all your friends and professional contacts. But the part I like is that you can also create a group list. Once you have created a group, you simply click on that group and your e-mail is automatically addressed to everyone in that group. I have my very close friends in one group. They are the people who know *everything* about my life. I have a list for general friends. These are people whom I believe will be interested in what is going on in my life, but I may not want them to know everything. I have a list of family members' e-mail addresses because I may want to send a note that would apply only to my immediate family. I have a list of cousins, some of whom I have stayed in touch with via e-mail while they lived outside the United States. We are not close enough that we would have taken the time to pen a letter and pay the extra postage to keep in touch, but through e-mail international communication is as easy as communicating with someone next door—and no more expensive!

I like to use e-mail as a form of journal keeping. When something really good, or really bad, happens in my life, I find that I sit down to write a few lines to update my friends and, before I know it, I have written several pages. Often this starts as an answer to the question of one friend. After I have written her a detailed, sometimes teary or gut-wrenching response, I think, "My other friends should know about this too!" Using the typical cut and paste method on the computer, I copy the information I just sent to the friend who asked the question. I then create a new e-mail message and paste in the epistle. I go through the address book and select the individuals or groups I think would be interested in this mail and hit the send button. My mail is gone. In a short time, it arrives in the e-mail box of everyone I sent it to. Frequently, if I am on-line for an extended length of time, I get a response before I even sign off!

Former *Los Angeles Times* columnist and Christian author Russ Chandler gave me this suggestion for anyone who is sending e-mail to many people. "When sending an e-mail to multiple persons and you don't want a long list to appear at the top, and/or you don't want to have everyone on the list know who else is receiving the message, put parentheses marks around the beginning and ending addresses in your header: (ERChandler), (MLittauer) for example." By doing this the recipient only knows that they got the mail and that it was sent to many, but they do not know whom. This also keeps the e-mail addresses of your friends private.

Another helpful tip regarding e-mail came to me from Paula Johnson. She wrote, "One of the niftiest e-mail tips is the fact that a person can compose one, to as many more as one wishes, e-mail letters off-line, then go on-line and mail them all at once. Perhaps many people already know this, but I have come across those who did not know it. This certainly beats taking up phone time while typing correspondence!" This is how I send my long journals to my friends. I usually compose them at home where I only have one phone line. While I am on-line, others cannot call in and no one else can use the phone.

With my enthusiasm for e-mail, I felt the need to bring my parents up to speed. My father has a laptop computer he uses when he travels. Since my parents are on the road most of the time, often in different time zones and with full schedules, they can be difficult to track down. E-mail is the perfect solution. All day long we can e-mail them questions, give them an important phone message, or advise them of a schedule change. All my father has to do is check in with his e-mail every night. After reading the note, he simply hits "reply" and types in his response. Next time we check in, there is his answer. Hardly a day goes by that I don't discover that another friend or acquaintance is now on-line.

My friend Connie Swanson brings up the need to make e-mail friendly. She comments, "Knowing that e-mail is for brief and fast communication didn't prepare me for the emotionless response. I misunderstood intent because of what seemed missing in content. There is more room for misunderstanding than with other forms of communication that are supported by eye contact or a voice or handwritten word." E-mail is often a conversational form of communication. But since it is actually written, a series of codes have developed to allow the writer to express emotion that would be heard with the spoken word. These codes are usually called smileys or emoticons. The basic smiley looks like this (tip your head slightly to the left as you look at it):

$$:-) \quad or \quad :)$$

Typically, a colon makes up the eyes and a dash is the nose. Other symbols are added or substituted to resemble an expressive face. Since the nature of e-mail is to be brief, these smileys can prevent a short statement from appearing terse or rude. Use them at the end of a sentence, one or two spaces after the period. If you are sending e-mail to someone who is new to the medium, you may need to explain these symbols the first time you use them. Otherwise they may think you cannot type!

While e-mail removes much of the formality of a written letter, there are some other tips that will help it be most effective—especially when using e-mail for professional correspondence.

Realize that many people get lots of e-mail, much of it junk. When you open up your incoming e-mail box, each unread item has the screen name of the sender and a "subject line." The subject line is important, because many people who get a lot of e-mail will only open some of them. Unless you know the recipient of your e-mail very well, do not put something basic like "Hello" in the subject line. It is suggested that an e-mail have only one subject, which makes it easy to reference later and to respond. The subject line should be concise, no more than six words. Your word choice sets the tone for the e-mail and helps the reader decide whether or not to read the mail now or later. You should phrase the subject line so that it includes both what the subject is and what you want the reader to do about it. Author James Scott Bell suggests, "Just as newspapers use headlines to draw your attention quickly, so should your short messages. Try to write a provocative headline in the 'subject' area of e-mail or fax, and *then* make your *first* sentence tie in to that."

Stephen Moss is the webmaster for his local government site in England. In that position he gets large volumes of e-mail from all over the world. He suggests, "E-mails should be short; nobody wants to read huge e-mails. They should get straight to the point. It is also very important to make sure that the content is unambiguous; something that you consider as humorous may not come over to the reader as that at all. When I send somebody an e-mail I expect a very fast reply. I always reply immediately to e-mails, even if it is only an acknowledgment to inform the person that their request will take some time to answer. I also ask them to e-mail me back if they haven't heard from me in a number of days; this lets them know that I don't consider their e-mail an intrusion." Cheryl Grounds e-mailed me this tip: "Just like any correspondence, return e-mail and faxes as soon as possible. Nothing irritates me more than to have to wait for days or weeks for a reply. Especially in the business world, this fast mode of communication should make life easier. I do not have the time to continually ask for a reply, to follow up with a telephone call. A lot of people are traveling with laptops now, so communication from a hotel room, airplane, etc. is just a matter of plugging everything in (if it works!)."

To make your e-mail most effective and take advantage of its quick nature, make it easy for the reader to read and respond. While the amount of type you can fit into an e-mail message is almost unlimited, the size of the screen is not. In her book, *Effective Business Writing*, Maryann Piotrowski suggests that you organize your message so that the most important message fits on the first screen. She says, "If your message goes on to the second or third screen, earlier screens are no longer visible to your reader. Avoid long messages."[1] Additionally, she suggests wording your message in such a way that the reader can respond with a simple "Yes" or "No" or a short response. When I read through my e-mail, the ones who have done this usually get a return e-mail from me the same day. Those whose message requires a long or involved answer get passed over because I do not have time to deal with it right then. I try to respond within a week, but depending on my schedule, it may be even longer. For these types of messages, the phone may be a better and faster form of communication. If you send an e-mail requiring a long, involved response, I suggest that you include your phone number.

When you answer e-mail, all you have to do is click on the reply button and the new message is already addressed to the sender. Even if you send the response back right away, the recipient might not get to it for a few days. By the time they read it, they may have forgotten what they had sent to you. Built into most e-mail systems is an automatic "quote" feature which makes it easy for the recipient to follow the train of thought. To use this feature, all you do is highlight the relevant text, then click on "reply". The new message automatically includes the selected text with a > symbol on the left, so the recipient can remember what he or she said and read your response. The new lines you type appear without the angled bracket.

Remember, as *The Vest Pocket Guide to Business Writing* says, "e-mail is a powerful, extremely accessible communication tool, so make it work for you. Writing action oriented e-mail is a critical skill that will help you get results—and reach more people faster than ever before."[2] You can e-mail me at MLittauer@aol.com, but please make it easy to respond! :)

Part Three

&

Speaking of Speaking

eight

How to Give an Introduction
∾
FLORENCE

Have you ever wondered how to introduce two people to each other? There they stand facing each other with you in between, all feeling somewhat awkward. Who is this unknown person?

There is an invisible wall between these two and you are the one to break it down. You have the opportunity of bringing two people together who don't know each other and opening up a possible future relationship, a networking opportunity, or at least a topic of momentary conversation. Being the new person in town, in church, or in a social group brings out feelings of insecurity; and such an individual is hoping for a rescuer who will break down those walls between him or her and the other happily conversing people in the room.

Introducing Others

The principles of a good introduction are valid for any kind of introduction, whether you are at a social gathering, introducing a new employee around the office, bringing a friend to a class, introducing a speaker, or even introducing yourself. Whether the introduction is one-on-one, one to a whole

119

group, or one to an audience, the principles are the same. The steps follow a simple outline: who, what, where, and why.

1. Who

"It is a pleasure for me to introduce my friend, my sister, my new next-door neighbor, my husband's mother...." After identification, give the name clearly. If there is anything unusual about the name that will make it easier to remember include this. "Littauer is an unusual name and it helps me to think of it as a tower with lights in it—a lit tower."

People don't grasp names quickly or remember them well, so repeat the name as often as is natural. Explain your relationship to this person in order to make a connection. "Some people avoid their mother-in-law but I have been blessed with an exceptional woman who has become my good friend." "Mary and I first met when trying on clothes at Macy's. I thought anyone with such good taste should be a friend of mine."

2. What

Once you have quickly established name and relationship, move on to some identification of what this person does, what interests she has, something that will open up conversation. "Sue teaches our Bible study and counsels women with marriage problems." (Sue will be popular immediately.) "Judy just won the club tennis match." "Rhonda has twin boys in my son's class."

The desire is to mention some quality, job, or honor that will give the other person something to converse about. If you just give the name and walk off, the two are left looking at each other with the question, "Where do we go from here?" But as you bring additional details about the person's life into the introduction, you create points of contact, areas that the listeners will want to bring up to start a conversation.

At a party for which she was the hostess, Marita realized that three men there, husbands of her friends, were into classic cars. Understanding the importance of a good introduction, she introduced them to one another, pointing out their shared interest. Suddenly this party full of people whom they did not know became much more interesting to them. They now had a common bond that they could chat about. The common bond was there all along, but without a good introduction, they would never have found each other. They might have remained bored, each accompanying his wife to a party of her friends.

3. Where

Many times people make connections when they find out where the new person lived previously. "Bev and Bill just moved here from New Haven, Connecticut, where he was on the faculty at Yale." Suddenly there's interest. "Oh, my sister lives in New Haven and her son is at Yale right now."

"Jane is from Houston, where she was a member of the First Baptist Church." "Did you happen to know Jim Johnson? He taught Sunday school there." Seldom does the person know Jim, but by mentioning where they're from you open up possibilities for a conversation. Remember, the function of an introduction is not just to show good manners but to make a connection between two or more people.

4. Why

We don't need to explain why we brought our friend with us, but if there is an interesting reason, it would be helpful to mention it. "Ellie doesn't know a soul in town and I thought the church supper was a great place to start." "Pam has a great interest in the Old Testament, so I knew she'd enjoy this class."

Once we understand how simple it is to introduce a friend, there should be no hesitation or awkward moments.

Introducing a Speaker

What if you are called upon to introduce the speaker at the spring luncheon? What do you do? Just as I've described above. Some speakers have a special introduction that they send ahead; your job is then to read it in such a lively way that it sounds as if you put it together. Assuming that you need to create the introduction, you should call the speaker's home or office ahead of time or depend upon a quick meeting with the speaker that day. You will be able to do this on a moment's notice if you remember who, what, where, and why.

Who: "Our speaker today is a delightful lady who entertained me during our lunch together."

What: "She told me stories about her children that made me want to meet them, all nine of them. The four of hers, the three of his, and the two of theirs."

Where: "Mrs. Baker comes to us from Boston, where she trained at Lesley College as a kindergarten teacher. I'm sure her training has come in handy with her own family."

Why: "Mrs. Baker is well qualified to speak to us today on raising children, as she has had more practical experience than most of us. Her sense of humor throughout her years as the mother of a blended family and her ability to see the Lord's hand on her life combine to make Mrs. Baker a fascinating speaker. We are grateful that she has taken time from her busy schedule to uplift us today. So help me welcome Becky Baker."

Now that you know how easy it is to introduce a speaker, volunteer to do it every time! How we, who are the speakers, hope for someone who cares and who will give us a positive, enthusiastic introduction. Remember, your job is to break down that invisible wall between the speaker on the platform and the audience below. You provide that bridge between the two. Some in the audience were dragged there and have little interest in the subject; and some are indifferent to life in general. Your introduction is not to be a list of schools the speaker attended (such details are probably in the printed program), but a brief enticement to make even the least-passionate person there excited about the prospects.

Always end with the equivalent of "so help me welcome Becky Baker" and then start the applause. The clapping fills in the pause between your introduction and the speaker's opening line. Plus, it generates a positive beginning to the speaker's presentation.

As a speaker, I send an introduction ahead, but at least 50 percent of the time it has somehow been lost and some frenzied lady runs up to tell me she has just been told to introduce me. If this woman happens to be you, I would have no problem. You would know just what to do.

I could write a book of different introductions I've been

given, including some in which my name is never mentioned. My favorite is the following, given by a pastor on a Sunday morning: "Our speaker today is not a real preacher and what you're going to hear is not a real sermon. In fact our speaker is wearing a dress, but listen anyway and don't be deceived by her packaging."

Many years ago, my husband was introduced to speak at a men's breakfast. At that time he hadn't written any books and the introduction went like this: "Our speaker today is Fred Littauer. His wife, Florence, has written many books, his daughter Lauren has written one book, and his daughter Marita has written three. It makes me wonder if perhaps we don't have the wrong Littauer here today!" With that he waved at Fred, who then had to rise to the occasion and begin.

It is unfair to any speaker to be introduced poorly, yet there is no school for professional introducers. Now that you have read this chapter you can be that one bright light in the next speaker's life.

Introducing Yourself

Have you ever been in a group situation in which someone decides that you should go around the room and all introduce yourselves? Have you seen the look of panic that passes over each face? Intelligent people suddenly don't know their own names. "There's really nothing much to say about me," some mumble.

But not you! From here on, you state clearly and with a smile the four Ws that you have sitting ready in your mind.

Identify who you are, what you do in life, where you live, and why you're there. One tip for introducing yourself, is to include your name last. Think about the last time you met someone new. You probably heard their name first. However, since you had other things on your mind, you were not really listening too carefully. As more was said about the person, you realized she was interesting. Now you wonder, "What was her name?" When you introduce yourself to a group or an individual, list the interesting details first, then conclude with, "My name is..." People will remember you much better with the information in that order.

Take a few minutes now to think about the Ws and how they apply to your life. Store a few facts about yourself in your mind, then when you are called upon to introduce yourself, you'll be ready. You will instantly be the star of the show because you spoke quickly and with confidence. It takes so little to be above average.

If you wish to help your children or any group you belong to in giving introductions of themselves or others, teach them the four Ws. Then have them practice on themselves and then on each other. At our CLASSeminars, we pair off people around the lunch table on the first day. Then each person interviews the person next to her and then introduces that person to the table. For some this is simple, but others have never done an introduction before and are delighted to know how easy it really is. Later that day, as we divide the attendees into small groups of ten, they have the opportunity to introduce themselves to their new friends. This exchange of personal information gets them all acquainted quickly and by the end of the third day some say this sharing time is the highlight of the seminar. One lady said, "I know more about the women in this group than I know about members of my own family."

People everywhere are hungry for personal relationships. Introduce yourself. The world needs to know you!

nine

The ABCs of Public Communication
∾
MARITA

R eport after report lists public speaking as one of the top fears of most Americans. According to anxiety expert Dr. Murray Stein of the University of California at San Diego, that fear is shared by 50 to 75 percent of women.[1] All through school most people feel terror at the mere thought of having to give an oral report. As adults, their palms sweat and their knees shake when they have to stand up and give a report or teach a lesson in their Sunday school class.

However, in spite of the grim reports, there are many people who think that being a speaker would be fun and glamorous. They hear the applause, watch the accolades, and covet the attention. For the past seventeen years, I have been involved in training people to improve their communication skills for both the spoken and written word through our CLASSeminar. While the concepts presented in the program will help everyone in their communication skills, the majority of those in attendance want to be speakers. Over the years we have trained approximately ten thousand men and women to be speakers. That is a big number when you consider that public speaking is a fear for most people.

Then there are people, perhaps you are among them, who do not desire to be a speaker, but who have had it thrust upon them. Maybe something dramatic has happened in your life and, as a result, people have invited you to share your story with their group. In many cases, churches are short of people willing to teach Sunday school and you get drafted. At the CLASSeminar, people often share that they feel God is pushing them "kicking and screaming" to some type of public platform. However you get there, willingly or unwillingly, there are numerous people who end up on some sort of stage. If you feel that God has done something in your life that you are so excited about that you cannot keep quiet, public speaking is one of the most effective and rewarding ways to communicate your passion.

Regardless of why we are there, when we look at the arena of "public" communication, one of the first things we need to look at is our motivation. Why do we want to be in the public? When we embark on public communication, we put ourselves in a position of leadership and set ourselves up for more extreme scrutiny than others face. James 3:1 tells us that not many of us should be teachers as we will be judged more harshly than the rest.

After spending the past twenty years of my life speaking to women's, church, and business groups I can attest to the validity of this verse. When you stand up in front of an audience, you become a target for anyone who disagrees with you. I am always amazed at the one person in one thousand who feels compelled to confront me with his or her negative perception of what I have said.

I have learned many lessons the hard way as I stood in front of a crowd and shared my heart. I remember one particularly difficult letter I received after speaking all weekend at a women's retreat. It was two pages long, handwritten in small print. As I opened it and glanced at the first few lines I could tell this was not going to be the typical "thank you for sharing with us" letter. As I read I felt the growing knot in my stomach get tighter and tighter. The gist of the letter was that I had not used enough Scripture in my presentations. Having learned to weigh all criticisms for validity, I went back through my notes.

I had presented four different messages throughout the weekend. Throughout those messages I had used thirty-eight different Bible verses. I was surprised at how high that number was because I am more of a biblical principles motivational speaker than a "Bible teacher." However, as I shared the various Scripture passages, I had either memorized them or read the verses from my notes. I never read them from the actual physical Bible. I can only assume that, since I did not hold the Bible throughout the entire presentation, that it was perceived that I did not use it. In reviewing the situation, I acknowledged that the comment was not something I needed to take to heart. But it still hurt. And, it did make me rethink my speaking and for what types of events my style would be the most appropriate.

Attitude

If our goals and purposes in being a speaker are not pure, facing these difficulties will wear us down and burn us out. I believe that the first thing we need to look at is our attitude. Attitude is the *A* in the ABCs. Our attitude is our inner feelings, our motivation for being up front.

As Christians our ultimate goal in life should be to be like Christ. The same is true for those of us who are Christian communicators: we want to model ourselves after Christ. As we search God's Word, looking at the life of Christ, we see that he had the attitude of a servant. In Matthew 20:28 Christ says, "Your attitude must be like my own, for I, the Messiah, did not come to be served, but to serve, and to give my life as a ransom for many" (LB). That commandment is reiterated in Luke 22:27, where he says, "Out in the world the master sits at the table and is served by his servants. But not here! For I am your servant" (LB). In the story of the Last Supper, Jesus served his disciples by performing a task usually reserved for the hired help. In John 13:14-15, he says, "And since I, the Lord and Teacher, have washed your feet, you ought to wash each other's feet. I have given you an example to follow: do as I have done to you." (LB). Clearly, we are to have the attitude of a servant!

As a speaker with the attitude of Christ, the attitude of a servant, we will be willing and even happy to help out wherever and whenever it is needed. I started speaking professionally when I was just nineteen years old. At that time my mother gave me some advice that I found very helpful and that I now pass on to you. She said, "Marita, you need to consider yourself in the employment of the person who invited you, or hired you, from the moment you get out of your car or off the plane, to the moment you get back in your car or on the plane."

Many times I have arrived early at the church where I was to speak and found the chairperson in a panic. Perhaps someone was sick or had forgotten to do a task. Occasionally, they had planned poorly and everything was not ready as they had hoped. Regardless of the reason, there is often work that still needs to be done at the last minute. Following Christ's example, and my mother's advice, I have joined in and helped with whatever task was at hand. I have stapled packets and set tables. Simply lending a hand can help set the tone for the entire event as it helps calm the nervousness the committee is experiencing and builds an instant rapport with the team.

One of the times I remember most clearly was when the event was held in the cafeteria of the local junior college. Part of the rental agreement the church had with the college was that the ladies had to do all the cleanup, leaving the room as they found it. When the event was over the women on the committee set about moving chairs and tables. While they were busy with that task, I packed up my book table and materials. As I finished, they were beginning to sweep the floors of the massive room. The lady who was in charge of taking me back to the hotel was also on the cleanup committee. I could have sat down and watched them sweep, but without thinking about it, I picked up a broom and began to sweep, too. I remembered that I need to consider myself in the employ of the people who invited me from the moment I arrive until I leave.

Bearing

Next we will look at the *B*, the bearing. The bearing is the outward display of that inner attitude. It is how we come across in our one-on-one interactions with people, not just those in attendance at the event, but the person taking care of us, the bellmen, and the skycaps.

Matthew 5:16 says, "Make your light shine, so that others will see the good that you do and will praise your father in heaven." For those of us who communicate publicly, this verse is a reminder that people are always watching us. We need to be sure that everything we do is a shining light so that others will see the good. We are an example, and people watch us! After attending one of our CLASSeminars Cindy Miller wrote, "It is so nice to be around people who are obviously quite successful in their ministries, yet have time for ordinary people."

Anyone can put on a good act on the stage for an hour. But if we have the right attitude and are authentic, people will be able to see that in us. However, for them to be able to see the real person, we must be willing to interact and mingle with the people in attendance. The bearing comes through when we are at all of the sessions of an event, rather than staying secluded in a side room.

My friend speaker and author Marilyn Heavilin was a part of the CLASSeminar teaching team for many years. She developed as a speaker during that time, and hearing the teaching on the ABCs was a part of that process. At all of her speaking engagements, Marilyn meets with the people and gets acquainted with them—even before she speaks. She has spoken at many large conferences sponsored by an international ministry. The first few times she was with this group, they showed her to the "speaker room," told her they would come and get her when it was time for her to speak, and left her there alone. Since she was new with this group, she followed the "rules" the first few times. However, while she sat there alone, she was wanting to be out with the people, talking with them and finding out what they needed. After a few times of seclusion, Marilyn got bolder. She told them that she wanted to be out with the people. The woman in charge was surprised because most of the speakers she had worked with did not want to mix with the people. As Marilyn got out into the crowd and mingled with the people, their reaction as an audience to what she had to say improved. She had already built a rapport with them.

Sometimes speakers will say that they need time alone before they speak to pray or prepare. However, if you are a pro, if you know what you are doing, all that should be done before you get there. When you arrive at a speaking engagement, you should be prayed up and you should be prepared! Then you can give the people in attendance all of your attention.

One year, at the Southern California Women's Retreat, I received a note from a woman that thrilled me and broke my heart at the same time. The note said, "This is the first Christian event I have been to where the speakers mingled with the peons—and I liked it!" Her comments thrilled me as I believe this is important. I was glad that she had noticed and that I plan this retreat in such a way that the speakers are available. We have a staff meeting Friday afternoon before the retreat starts. I tell all my speakers that I expect them to be there for all the sessions, that there is no reserved seating for the speakers, and that they should sit with different attendees at each meal. I want them to be at their book tables during all the breaks to sign books and talk with the attendees. So, I was pleased that someone had noticed and appreciated it enough to go out of the way to comment on it. (People usually only go out of their way to comment on the negatives.) But her comments broke my heart because she said, "this is the *first* Christian event..." This should be standard; every speaker should mix with the people, just like Christ did. Her word choice of *peons* also concerned me. When we have the attitude of a servant, our bearing should never make anyone feel like a peon. The audience is the reason for our existence as a speaker; they should be lifted up, not us.

Clothing

The *C* of the ABCs is clothing. It is mentioned last because it is not the most important element, but it has importance nonetheless.

You have probably heard the cliché, "You never have a second chance to make a good first impression." It is a cliché because it is universally true. However, for those of us who communicate publicly, it is especially true. Look back on speakers you have heard in the past. As they walked across the stage to take the microphone, didn't you look at them and make a quick assessment before they even opened their mouths? If there was a picture on the brochure or flyer announcing the event, it may have helped you decide whether or not to attend. It is human nature to make a physical assessment.

As I teach this material at the CLASSeminar, I ask the attendees if, as the staff all lined up to introduce themselves that morning, they had looked at us and made some kind of assessment about us. Perhaps they had looked at us and said to themselves, "Oh, she looks fun, I hope I am in her group," or

"She looks like I'd like her." They all raise their hands in agreement that, yes, they had made some kind of decision about us based solely on the way we were dressed and the way we looked. This is why our clothing is important.

It is true that, as it says in 1 Peter 3:3, we should not depend on clothing or jewelry for our beauty. However, many Christians have taken this to mean that our "outer adornment" should be ignored altogether. When we stand up in front of a group, we are in a position of leadership and Scripture points out the use of special clothing to indicate a position of honor or leadership. In Exodus 26–31, God is instructing Moses on the building of the tabernacle. In 28:2 he gives specific directions for Aaron's clothing: "Make special clothes for Aaron, to indicate his separation to God—beautiful garments that will lend dignity to his work" (LB). Aaron was the high priest, the spiritual leader of the nation of Israel and he needed special clothing that set him apart. As speakers, as leaders, we need to dress in such a way as to lend dignity to our work.

In Luke 15, the story of the prodigal son, the son has just come home. In his joy, the father wants to have a celebration feast. Verse 22 says, "Quick! Bring the finest robe in the house and put it on him. And a jeweled ring for his finger and shoes!" (LB) The fine clothes set him apart and indicated his position of honor.

Likewise, we as speakers need to have special clothes when we stand in front of an audience. At the CLASSeminar we suggest that you dress one notch above the audience, not because you think you are better than they are, but because you are in a position of leadership. We suggest that you find out how the audience will be dressed and then go one step beyond that. For example, if you are going to speak to a businesswomen's luncheon, they will probably all be in dresses and business suits. As the speaker, you should wear a suit. Not a navy blue suit with a white blouse, but something special, something that has style and makes a statement. If you are speaking for a women's retreat at a Christian conference center in the woods, most people will be dressed in jeans and sweatshirts. As the speaker, you should wear slacks and a sweater— one notch above. We once got a negative evaluation on a speaker who was in a rustic environment but wore sweaters with sequins and silk pants. Her dress set her too far apart and the people felt they could not relate to her.

It has been said that if you walk like a leader, talk like a leader, and look like a leader, people will follow you. Our clothing separates us and puts us in that position of leadership and helps us make a good first impression. The Appendix features many additional helpful tips for dressing for the platform.

Remember, as a speaker you are always on stage. But, as a Christian it is not just an act, but a matter of attitude. Your goal is to change lives and to be a servant, not to be a star.

ten

Developing Your Topic
ᴄᴡ
MARITA

Most people get interested in public speaking because something dramatic has happened in their lives that is "sharable." This is a good place to get started. When you share your story, you do not have to do much research; you know your life. You do not need to organize or outline very much because a story is usually told in chronological order.

Other people get involved in public speaking through Bible teaching, leading a group by using a study guide. Minimal research and organization is needed here because the writer of the study has done the work for you.

Both the testimony or Bible teaching approaches are effective. However, in recent years, things have changed. People's lives have become very busy and complex. Many women work outside the home. When their careers are combined with their household obligations and personal responsibilities, they no longer have time to go to a meeting just to hear a nice story. The lives of women whose focus is their home have become increasingly full. With fewer women available to assist in the volunteer positions, the stay-at-home mom is feeling stretched and pulled. An event needs to offer more than free child care to get them to commit the time.

Whether the event for which you may be speaking is a Bible

a ladies' luncheon, the increasing expectation is that these meetings must offer solid take-home value. Through CLASS, we represent over one hundred different gifted Christian communicators. Churches, schools, and businesses from all over the country call us, looking for speakers to meet the needs of their various programs. We have been actively offering this service for over ten years. While there have been some subtle shifts in the topics the groups are seeking, virtually no one who calls looking for a speaker says, "we just want a nice story or a good Bible lesson." Typically, the meeting planner, often a women's ministry director, has sensed a need in the lives of her women. She calls us looking for someone who can meet that specific need.

There is nothing wrong with having a story to tell or being a Bible teacher. However, I hope to encourage you to broaden your topic base, to go beyond the basics. If you tell your story well or you are a gifted Bible teacher, you will find that people assume you have additional areas upon which you can speak. They will invite you to do more. You will then need to develop your topics.

Whether you are already speaking publicly or are just starting out and are looking for help, you can begin to develop your topics by looking to your own life experiences. Each of us is unique. We have different things that make us who we are.

At the CLASSeminar we call these aspects of our lives, our "seeds of interest." The following is a listing of topics that may be areas you could develop. To help you see how a specific subject could be used, I have selected the topic description from the information sheets of many of the speakers we represent. When I am working with a speaker, or potential speaker,

I find that reviewing the topics other speakers are addressing helps them see how different themes could be developed. You do not steal or copy their ideas; but rather, you allow what they are doing to inspire ideas of what you could do with your interests and expertise.

As you review the suggested topics, place a check mark in the space provided for each description that hits home. For example, I do not have a degree in home economics, but when I was a child my father was in the restaurant business. My mother is an excellent cook. We had guests in our home frequently and all of us learned to cook. So cooking, entertaining, and hospitality are important parts of my life. When I review the suggested topics, I check off hospitality.

As you review the following "seeds of interest," remember that this is *not* an all-inclusive list. It is designed to be a starting place, to help you expand your potential topics. Later we will address what to do with the ideas once you begin to plant the seeds in your mind.

Personal Interest

Mental Health

____ *Depression*
Mental Health and a Transformed Life (Jaque Banas)
Jackie exposes how most people's problems are rooted in poor thinking and will offer keys to unlock their "brain shackles" and remove their mental blindfolds.

____ *Stress*
It's Time to De-Stress (Cheryl Townsley)
Knowing the many faces (symptoms) of stress can help you accurately pinpoint the roots of your stress, which can include a hectic schedule, your environment, finances, emotional pressures, and poor nutrition. Cheryl will help you de-stress.

____ *Emotional Problems*
Balancing Your Emotions (Gayle Roper)
What are seven things that might give a woman difficulties with her emotions? Gayle will give you six keys to learning to control your ups and downs in spite of circumstances. Based on her book by the same title.

____ *Phobias*
Phobics Victorious (Rosemary Hartman)
Has fear affected your life and your choices? Has your self-concept been marred by past hurts, rejections, and abandonment? Have despair and depression kept you from the joy of the Lord? If you can answer "yes" to any of these questions, then the topics of this presentation are for you!

____ *Suicide*
How to Teach Your Child to Fail (Angie Mitchell)
Suicide is the leading cause of death among young people. In this presentation, problem-solving skills, stress management, and coping skills are shared so that parents, teachers, and other youth workers can answer a desperate cry for help.

____ *Compulsions*
Grace and Addiction (Terry Webb)
Based on her book, *Tree of Renewed Life,* Terry traces the Christian origins of the 12-Step movement and how this spiritual program is similar to but different from Christian religious tradition and doctrine. She will answer the questions, "How is God's grace related to recovery from addiction?" and "Can one achieve healing from addiction without the 12 Steps?"

Physical Fitness

____ *Weight Control*
The Buddy System Seminar (Lille Diane)
After losing sixty pounds, Lille went to work for a major weight-loss company but missed sharing with others how her personal buddy, Jesus, had been the key to her weight-loss success. Seeing a need, Lille developed the Buddy System, complete with sixteen weeks of teaching topics, spiritual encouragement, support, and fun.

____ *Exercise*
My Body, My Temple (Laurie Ellsworth)
A practical and motivational presentation on how to be healthy and fit during every season of your life. Discover four key techniques that are absolute essentials in nutrition and physical activity.

____ *Diet and Nutrition*
Cooking for Health (Kathleen O'Bannon Baldinger)
Do menus with more vegetables and less fat boggle your mind? Kathleen will demonstrate the easy way to cook with foods that you suspect are part of a healthy diet but may never have tried before.

Spiritual Interests

____ *Bible Study*
The Motions of Devotions (Tami McGrew)
Tami has one passion—to create Bible students who can open the Bible and find the doctrine or direction they need. With instruction on how to use available study tools, Bible symbols, and a Spirit-guided imagination, this presentation will get people moving with a plan for daily Bible study.

____ *Teaching*
Learning to Lead (Elizabeth George)
The church is in desperate need of leaders. While many are willing, few have the tools or training to be effective. As a result, those who do come forward to fill the needs often burn out and give up. Yet with some basic training, efforts can be rewarding for everyone. If you desire to lead women or are already in that position, this session will offer valuable tips and energize your mission.

____ *Lay Counseling*
What to Say When (Dennis and Ruth Gibson)
The Gibsons have dozens of techniques you can use if you find people asking you for personal help, and you only have a brief opportunity. Based on Dennis' book *Vitality Therapy*.

____ *Spiritual Gifts*
Essences Within (Ruth Hansen)
Rediscover, develop, and use the spiritual gifts God has planted within you. You can bring wholeness and holiness to members of your congregation.

____ *Prayer*
Prayer: Life's Ultimate Privilege (Shirley Lindsay)
Do you desire a closer relationship with the Lord? Have you attended seminars offering ten easy steps to a successful prayer life but found they don't work for you? Shirley's fresh approach to a closer relationship with God focuses on prayer as life's ultimate privilege. You will discover and experience the dynamics of a powerful prayer life.

____ *Church Administration*
Growing your Church from Fifty to Five hundred (Philip Wagner)
Studies show that about 85 percent of all American churches have an attendance of two hundred people or less and that 80 percent of all churches are either on a plateau or in decline. Learn biblical and practical principles to help you and your staff prayerfully lead a growing church.

_____ *Emotional Healing*
This Old House ... Remodeling or Restoration (Dolley Carlson)
In this talk, Dolley likens our hearts and souls to a house. Are you remodeling by applying temporary fix-ups? Or are you ready for restoration through returning to God the Father's original plan for you?

_____ *Angels*
A Rustle of Angels (Marilynn Carlson Webber)
Discover who angels are, what they are like, what they do, and the ministry they perform in your life right now. Don't let the secular promotion of cute little cherubs scare you away from the full understanding and blessings of one of God's provisions.

_____ *Spiritual Warfare*
Spiritual Warfare of the Heart (Jim Lucas)
Most of us tend to think of spiritual warfare as "out there": political issues, prayer campaigns, revivals. While these are part of our warfare, Jim shows that often the most intensive warfare is in our own hearts and important relationships. He gives insight, practical steps, and hope for this warfare that will help you win where it counts.

_____ *Evangelism/Discipleship*
Discipleship: Changing the World One Person at a Time (Pam Farrel)
Keys to effective follow-up, basic discipleship, and leadership development. This seminar is aimed at motivating and training the average Christian woman to become a Titus 2 woman.

Personal Relationships

Friendship

_____ *Being a Friend*
The Sweet Gift of Friendship ... Kindred Spirits (Pam Stephens)
Friendship is like a garden: we prepare the soil, select the seed,

water and nourish, even weed and prune. It is hard work, but worth the effort for a lasting harvest. Sisterhood is a sweet gift that we can enjoy, especially if our expectations are realistic.

___ *Singles*
Single and Celebrating (Bob and Yvonne Turnbull)
Singles are in the continual process of building relationships, but often they don't have the tools necessary to create strong, lasting ones. This seminar enables singles to overcome these obstacles so they can build God-honoring relationships.

___ *Loneliness*
Intimate Moments: Getting Close to Those You Love (Karen O'Connor)
Look at and practice specific ways to cultivate more intimacy with God, with yourself, and with others. Take away practical and spiritual tools for deepening intimate relationships.

___ *Encouragement*
Real Angels Give Their Friends Wings (Linda Shepherd)
"We are like angels with just one wing. We can only fly embracing each other" (author unknown). Linda teaches how to encourage others and how to find and receive encouragement as well.

Marriage

___ *Meaning of Love*
Love Notes (Cheryl Kirking)
For couples' events, Cheryl shares anecdotes and original songs about love and marriage. Audience members will probably recognize themselves in many of the stories and will learn ways to improve communication. David Kilker, her husband of over thirteen years, often joins her in this presentation.

___ *Sexuality*
Woman's Sexuality (Mary Ann Mayo)
Mary Ann provides listeners with wonderful insight into the nature of feminine sexuality that will enliven and enrich relations

between husbands and wives, and liberate both from unrealistic expectations promoted by distortions of popular media. Upon request and schedule permitting, her husband, Dr. Joseph Mayo, a Stanford-trained ob/gyn with over twenty years' experience, speaks with Mary Ann.

____ *Marriage Preservation*
Preadultery ... What a Tangled Web We Weave (Vicky Olsen)
Why are so many Christian marriages falling prey to adultery? How do two couples who started out as friends find themselves entangled in a web of infidelity? Vicky explores some of the reasons for marital unfaithfulness and imparts biblical and practical tools for safeguarding your marriage.

____ *The Art of Marriage*
Marriage Alive Seminar (Dave and Claudia Arp)
Dave and Claudia's most-requested seminar is an exciting, fun-filled approach to building thriving marriages. Some of the topics covered are: prioritizing your marriage, finding unity in diversity, communicating feelings, processing anger and resolving conflict, and building spiritual intimacy.

Children

____ *General Advice*
Home Improvement (Colleen Mountain)
How are things on the home front these days? Colleen shares many secrets for carving time out of our over-committed '90s schedules to keep the "sweet" in home sweet home.

____ *Preschool Children*
Motivating Your Children From Crayons to Career (Cheri Fuller)
Cheri shares ways to motivate young people without undue pressure and stress. She teaches how to instill a joy for learning and a positive "can do" attitude needed for success in life—including how to encourage "late bloomers" and underachievers.

____ *Discipline*
Discipline Children Effectively (Kathy Collard Miller)
There are definite how-to's for effectively disciplining children. Kathy presents three levels of disciplining, and discusses the differences between punishment versus discipline, and willful disobedience versus childish irresponsibility.

____ *Communication*
Are There Villains in Your Home, Destroying Honest Communication? (M.J. MacPherson)
Who are those villains? What is their source? Can members of your family make you feel agitated, even unloved? Might you be a villain? M.J. will humorously illustrate four villains and share tools for healing relationships and making permanent, positive change!

____ *Teen Morality and Pregnancy*
True Love Waits (Karie Weston)
Temptation affects all of us. Karie shows how important it is to develop principles that will help in the "heat of passion." Students are challenged and encouraged in the areas of dating, sex, and self-image.

____ *Empty Nest*
Golden Girls (Rosa Maria Faulkner)
Do you feel ready for life on the Golden Pond? Will you sit out your golden years in the empty nest thinking that you have completed your service? This message from Titus 2 will inspire senior women to be true Golden Girls using their abilities, insight, and wisdom to nurture the younger women now.

____ *Grandparenting*
Grandma Calls Me Precious (Betty Southard)
Today, grandmothers are more active than ever before. Grandmothers can instill that priceless feeling of unconditional love and acceptance in their grandchildren. However, grandmothers can end up in the middle of some rather sticky situations. This message will equip both mothers and grandmothers to effectively handle any situation that presents itself with finesse and confidence.

Family

____ *Responsibility for Parents*
Full Circle (Joyce Minatra)
Watching our parents degenerate from dynamic people to infirmity is difficult. For those who care for their elderly parents, Joyce shares her experiences and encourages those who fight the relentless battle of exhaustion, frustration, and guilt. She shares how each of us can make it a happier time of life for everyone.

____ *Divorce*
Growing Through the Pain (Marjorie Lee Chandler)
You, a midlife parent, learn that your adult son or daughter is getting a divorce. God does not forsake you as you walk through emotional pain. Instead, he gives new insights.

____ *Overcoming Divorce*
He Is Able (Jo Franz)
Jo shares the steps she took to recover from an unwanted divorce after fifteen years of marriage. Unflinchingly honest and vulnerable, Jo will challenge you to go beyond where we so easily gravitate after divorce—into another relationship. You will leave this session with personalized tools that will give you hope for a future where God proves he is able to make you what he wants you to be.

____ *Single Parents*
Single Parents—Hats Off to You! (Pam Lehtonen)
Single parents have unique and complicated challenges. Pam understands what it means to be a single parent and will share how your unique obstacles can be turned into opportunities to strengthen your relationship with your children.

Suffering

____ *Coping*
Unwrapping the Gifts in Adversity (Georgia Shaffer)
Learning to cope and move beyond difficult losses such as

divorce, death, serious illness, or job termination is not easy. Georgia will introduce you to the five-step process she used when facing adversity.

___ *Sickness and Pain*
Four Tips to Survival (Tina Searcy)
Tina presents practical tips on dealing with and fighting disease, focusing on fighting the battle on all fronts: spiritual, physical, mental, and emotional. Her positive attitude will be an encouragement to people who are ill and to their family members.

___ *Death and Dying*
Healing for Heartaches (Sharon Marshall)
People tell us that, if we have enough faith, we will be victorious in every circumstance. Of course, it's true—but they often forget to tell us that time, struggle, and doubt are our usual companions on the road to victory. In these sessions, you will discover the normal process for dealing with loss.

___ *Other Issues*
Putting Your Fears to Rest (Holli Kenley)
Research tells us that 40 to 60 percent of all women from fifteen to fifty years of age experience PMS symptoms. A large number of women do not even know what is wrong with them. In this presentation, you will learn for yourself what PMS is all about.

___ *Recovery*
Bounce Back (Diana James)
This heartwarming message provides hope and encouragement to prepare us for, or help us through, times of disappointment, grief, failure, or fear. Diana shares spiritual insights and relates poignant, sometimes humorous, true stories of people who give God the glory for enabling them to "bounce back."

Personal Goals

Self-Improvement

_____ *Self-Image*
Making Friends With Yourself (Leslie Vernick)
Sometimes we are plagued with doubt, feelings of inferiority, and self-criticism. In this session you will learn where a negative self-image originates and to distinguish between biblical self-image and the popular notion of self-love.

_____ *Conversation*
Creative Charisma: Bringing Out the Best in Yourself and Others (Marita Littauer)
Does it seem like common courtesy has gone by the wayside? In this session you will learn about the qualities of Concern, Compliments, Conversation, Consent, and Companionship. When you bring out the best in others, you really are bringing out the best in you!

_____ *Creativity*
Created to Be Creative (Teri Messner)
You have been created to be creative. What do you have to offer that is uniquely your own? Teri's refreshing, encouraging, and inspirational message will help individuals find their own unique gifts.

_____ *Identity*
The Real Me (Lee Ezell)
A light hearted approach on how to lose feelings of inadequacy and intimidation so the "real you" can stand up! Based on her book, *Will the Real Me Please Stand Up?*

_____ *Color, Clothes, and Fashion*
Beauty and the Best (Rebecca Baker)
This seminar is packed full of tips accumulated from fifteen years of modeling. In addition, discover the best ways to fulfill 1 Corinthians 6:20—the honoring of God with your body.

____ *Beauty, Makeup, and Hair*
Ageless Beauty Secrets (Sharon Hoffman)
Firmly convinced that every woman, regardless of age, can be absolutely beautiful, Sharon discloses her "no fail" beauty secrets. In this session Sharon discusses how to learn to accept what cannot be changed and how to make the most of God's gifts to you. In contrast to current trends of aggressive sensuality, Sharon encourages beauty from within.

____ *Goals in Life*
Goal setting: Drawing a Target on the Wall (Kendra Smiley)
Setting goals is like drawing a target on the wall. You may not always hit the bull's-eye, but at least you will be facing the right wall! This presentation will provide you with the basic skills necessary for setting goals in all aspects of your life.

Leadership

____ *Qualities of a Leader*
Reaching Your Mountaintop: Developing Your Leadership Potential (Linda Olson)
Whether it is in your business, your home, or your work in the community, this seminar will teach you principles and concepts that will help you discover who you are, relate to others more effectively, work less and gain more, and enjoy the fruits of your labor.

____ *Political Issues*
Bridging the Gap (Jeff Crume)
Racism in any form is destructive. This workshop discusses how society, cultural conditioning, and peer pressure contribute to racism and how education and communication help resolve it.

Organization

___ *Household*
More Hours in My Day (Emilie Barnes)
This seminar is the answer to the cry "There aren't enough hours in my day!" This seminar is not just a brief organizational binge but a lasting lifestyle change.

___ *Personal*
The Time Game: Playing by God's Rules (Deb Haggerty)
As did the Proverbs 31 woman, today's busy woman will find that a life firmly grounded in the Word of God will enable her to manage her time and priorities in a manner pleasing to the Lord, her family, and her friends.

___ *Home Decorating*
Gracious Living (Susan Ponville)
Do you save fun and festivities for a small percentage of your life such as birthdays and holidays? Susan teaches you to celebrate each day by adding simple, distinctive touches. Susan will show you how to transform all areas of your home into lovely oases of tranquility.

___ *Working Women*
You, Too, Can Thrive as a Working Woman (Gwen Ellis)
Most working women have two jobs—one at their places of employment and the other at home. Based on her book *Thriving as a Working Woman,* Gwen's presentation offers ideas on everything from thriving as a harried cook to identifying and developing skills that could propel you forward in your job.

___ *Time Management*
Time Well Spent (Sue McMillin)
This time-management presentation is unique because it is for women only. Sue will bring practical applications to the unique issues that women face in managing their time.

____ *Hospitality*
Entertaining on a Shoestring (Bonnie Skinner)
Bonnie has always enjoyed entertaining and shares humorous stories and guidelines for entertaining and the importance of "being yourself."

Fill in your own ideas here:

_____

_____

_____

_____

_____

Did you find some topics that you could address? Some areas in which you have an interest, even if it is undeveloped? As you read through the various listings and saw how different people present a specific topic, I hope you have seen new areas you had not even thought of yet. Remember, there are hundreds of other topics on which you could speak. This listing is meant to expand your thinking.

Additionally, there are many different ways a subject can be addressed. As I reviewed the various information sheets of the speakers represented by CLASS to select the titles presented here, I found many different presentations on prayer and friendship, for example. Due to space limitations, I selected only one title for each topic. Please use these subjects only as a launching place for your own ideas, not a final answer. As you have reviewed these topics, I hope they have spurred your thinking on to new areas that were not even listed here. Be sure to jot them down as well.

If you did not check off the topics of interest to you, please go back and do that before moving on to the next chapter. In doing this exercise, Bonnie Skinner said, "I have found this to be my greatest source of material for my presentations. By honestly rating the appeal of each of the examples listed, I can analyze where I've been, where I am, and where I am going. This could possibly save a person a trip to therapy!"

We can all be grateful that what qualifies us to be Christian speakers is what God has done in our lives and our personal experiences, not the education we have or the degrees we hold.

eleven

Researching and Organizing Your Topic

∽

MARITA

Now that you have a collection of topics that interest you and that you have some level of experience in, you have a foundation upon which to build. It is time to begin to gather material that will support your "seeds of interest."

Through seventeen years of teaching these concepts, however, I have found that if you just collect "stuff," it merely adds to the chaos in your life. So, before you set to work researching your topics, I suggest that you create a system for organizing and storing the fruit of your research. When we know that we have a place to put things, we are much more apt to collect them.

Selecting a System

The exact details of the system will be determined by your available space and your personality. When I teach these concepts at the CLASSeminar, I find that those who are at least half Perfect are already very organized but may not have thought of organizing their research in this way. For the Populars, this is flexible enough that even we can do it.

Start by selecting the type of filing system you think will

work the best for you. My mother does not like to be con-
fined. Originally, she preferred the "throw it in a box"
method. She used the 8-1/2 x 11-inch boxes that printing or
copies came in. They were the perfect size and already had a
space on the side for labeling the contents.

Some people like the accordion files and others prefer the
traditional file folders. I suggest using file folders because they
are flexible and easily allow for growth. If, like me, you find
that once you have put something in a file folder, you can't
find it, I believe that you will find the few extra cents that colored file folders cost are well worth the investment. Those of
us who are at least half Popular tend to have a memory for
color. While we may not remember exactly which folder we
put something in, we will remember what color the file was.
When we have files of many colors, it narrows down how
many files we have to look through.

Once you have determined what type of system you are
going to use, go back over the previous chapter to see how
many of the topics suggested in the "seeds of interest" you
checked off. Add to that number any additional topics you
have added. Now go and purchase the needed items to make
your system. For example, if you checked off fifteen topics,
then make sure that you buy enough files or boxes, or an
accordion file with at least that many slots. Next, label each of
the files, boxes, or tabs with one of the topics you checked off
under the "seeds of interest."

Starting Your Research With Reading

Now you have your system ready to organize your research. Research does not mean that you have to go to the library or spend hours on the Internet. At this stage what we suggest is a passive research, being alert to life. Begin to look around you for anything that fits into one of your topics.

One the most obvious places to start your research are books, magazines, and newspapers. From now on, you want to be alert, reading everything, anywhere, at any time. You want to look for any articles, facts, quotes, or statistics that fit into your personal topics. Even if you think you are only mildly interested in a topic today, be on the lookout for anything that might address it. Note that every day, *USA Today* offers some quick facts on the bottom left-hand corner of the front page. Whenever you have a *USA Today* in your hands, check that out to see if the information provided there is anything you can use. Skim your local newspaper for articles on the topics of your interest. When you are at a doctor's office, on an airplane, or anywhere else that provides magazines for you to read, flip through the offerings—especially if their selection includes magazines to which you do not normally subscribe.

Even advertising may provide something that fits into your interests. One of my topics of interest is "Confidence." I found a long, narrow ad which stated at the top, "Tips, tricks and sound advice for increasing your self-confidence." Since this is one of my seeds of interest, the ad caught my eye. It offered five points. The first four are truly helpful hints. It suggests things such as smiling, wearing red lipstick, standing tall, and dressing creatively. The fifth point, however, says to protect your self-assurance by using a certain antiperspirant. I cut that ad out. When I speak on confidence I open with the world's view of confidence and I use that ad. I read off the first four points, illustrating them bodily—I stand tall, I smile, and of course I am dressed creatively. When I get to the antiperspirant, everyone laughs! Even ads can help develop your topic. Read everything, everywhere, at any time.

As you begin to train your mind to look for information that matches your interests, you will be amazed at how much is available without any aggressive work. As you are reading, mark any phrases, sentences, or paragraphs that fit your topic. Underline them with a colored pen so that they are easily identifiable at a later date. Additionally, make a notation of the corresponding topic in the margin and add any comments that the reading brought to mind. It is important to do this as you read.

I learned this the hard way. One night I was reading a book in bed. I read a section that I thought would fit in perfectly with one of my presentations. I reached to the night table to grab a pen, but there were none there. I was all warm and snuggly and did not want to get out of bed, so I folded that particular page in a special way that would identify that section when I got back to it. A few days later I had the book and the pen in my hand at the same time. I went back to that page. I read the front side. I read the back side. I read the page before it and the page after it. Whatever had struck me as so brilliant a few nights earlier was no longer there, or at least I could not find it. I was not in the same frame of mind as I had been when I had originally read it. If I had underlined and made a notation as I read, as I teach others to do, I would not have lost the quote I thought would enrich my presentation.

As you find things, cut them out. I suggest that you keep both a pocket knife or scissors and a colored pen with you at all times. Perhaps have one set in your purse and keep another set wherever you read. If you are reading a book, you may not want to cut it up. You can still collect the information by marking it as you read. Later, make a copy of the page or pages with the desired quote along with the title page and the copyright page. If you are reading from a newspaper or magazine, be sure to cut out not only the article you want, but also the name of the publication and the issue date. If you ever want to use that article in a speech, article, or book of your own, you will need the source information. For a newspaper, cutting off the top of the front page will give you the needed information. Most magazines include the magazine name and issue information on the bottom corner of every editorial page. If that information is not listed on the pages of the articles you cut out, the cover should give you what you need.

When you are cutting material out of magazines, we suggest that you not only cut out the article, but also the pull off the complete cover, both front and back, as one piece, if possible. The magazine cover acts like a folder to hold the article you have selected. It protects the article and provides a visual affirmation of the source. Lay the magazine cover open and then place the article inside. If the article starts with a two-page spread, take the left-hand side of the article and staple it into the left-hand side of the cover. For the remaining pages of the article, staple them on the top left side to the right side of the cover. When this is done correctly, the article should resemble the way it looked in the magazine.

After cutting out or copying the material, you are then ready to file your selections without the bulk of the entire publication. File your research into the waiting file folders titled with your seeds of interest.

Write It Down!

Another way to gather information is from your life and the observations you make. All of us have things that happen to us, both good and bad, that we think we will never forget. However, as time passes, we may remember that the event happened, but the specifics begin to grow fuzzy.

Keep paper and a pen or pencil with you at all times. As you see or hear something that fits your topic, write it down. You may hear other speakers who say something that you can quote. You may observe an interaction between a parent and a child that illustrates a point you wish to make. You may have an experience in which you learn a valuable lesson. Any of these incidents can add interest to your speaking and writing … if you can remember them! That is why writing them down is so important. These notes should also be added to your file folders under the appropriate topic. If you want to file something in two places, you can either make a copy of it, or place a note in one file to cross reference the other file.

Journaling is another wonderful way to gather material on your topics. Some people enjoy writing down the events of their lives on a daily basis. Others find the healthy release of writing down their thoughts, feelings, and emotions to be especially helpful when they are going through a difficult time.

Journaling is different from keeping a diary. A diary records events. A journal captures feelings. The specific feelings you are facing during a difficult time may be just the thing to add to your presentation to give it depth, emotion, and validity.

Patsy Clairmont was a part of our CLASS staff for ten years. In her book *Under His Wings,* she writes, "Journaling can expedite healing, because our hands are extensions of our hearts, and many times we will write what we wouldn't risk saying."[1]

Journaling helps us organize our thoughts. Often life's distractions can leave us feeling scattered. But when we take the time to sit and write, we can focus, and what is really important often becomes clear.

To get started, look at your day and write about something that happened that would make a great movie clip. Incorporate all your senses, so that when you read it later you will be able to see it, hear it, smell it, taste it, and feel it. Create a picture with words.

Journaling is something that has no wrong way. There are no "shoulds." Write what makes you feel comfortable, your "shoes-off" self. Georgia Shaffer, who often teaches about journaling at the CLASSeminar, teaches that, "one day you may write a sentence or paragraph. Another day, several pages. There are no rules. You don't have to write every day—make it fun. You don't have to write in complete sentences. There will be days you don't feel like doing it—so give yourself permission to skip that day." Whether you keep a journal daily or sporadically as needed, it is a great way to capture your feelings as you are going through a situation you may later want to relive or in some way reference—even if you do not completely understand the experience at the time.

I find that as a Popular personality, I do not have the discipline or time to journal every day. However, when I have been in the midst of a stressful situation, writing about what is going on and how I feel is a catharsis. For me, this usually takes place when a caring friend, who knows what I am facing, e-mails me and asks me how things are going. In writing an answer to her question, I often find that I have written five pages which allowed me to process my feelings while capturing them on paper.

Whether your journaling efforts take place on paper, on a computer, or in a pretty little blank book, the thoughts and feelings you write down should ultimately be transferred to the appropriate files or can be cross-referenced to the actual journals.

Keep Your Files Updated

Once you begin to speak on a topic, keep updating your files with new material. As you address a specific topic publicly, you may get letters from people on how that message helped them and met their needs. Keep these encouraging notes and place them in the appropriate files.

Speaker Bonnie Skinner tells how this system has helped her.

I was fifty-eight years old when I first attended the CLASSeminar. My life has always been full of exciting and interesting events. Through the years I had accumulated two or three boxes of newspaper and magazine clippings, plus an abundance of other things including wonderful memories of my life up to that point. My Popular personality overcame my occasional thoughts of organization and I had never taken the time to sort through my "Seeds of Interest." I didn't even know that's what they were until I attended the CLASSeminar. On my way home from the CLASSeminar, I stopped by Office Depot and purchased one hundred manila folders. As I began sorting through the newspaper and magazine clippings, I couldn't decide how to label the folders. After some deliberation, I decided to use the titles that were used in the Seeds of Interest section of the CLASSeminar Notebook. I surmised "If it's good enough for Florence Littauer, it's good enough for me!"

In short order, my one hundred folders were labeled. I used a cardboard box as my first "filing cabinet" and made one rule for filing: pick up the clipping and either file or toss. To my surprise every one of my articles found a home in an appropriate folder. That was the beginning of my filing system! I quickly advanced to a four-drawer filing cabinet and now I can easily access topics on any subject I need.

In my years as a military wife and mother of three, I never felt the need for my own filing cabinet. I had folders on marriage and homemaking, children, entertaining, and sightseeing (for when relatives came). My family came first for thirty-five years. The one thing I did during those years proved to be incredibly valuable: I continually filled my reservoir and created my own seeds of interest all the while. I didn't have time to read some of the articles but I did take time to save them because they appealed to me. Now that my responsibilities have changed (my husband is retired and enjoys his own interests), I very quickly got my act together (attending the CLASSeminar provided the impetus to set me on the right path) because the bulging folders immediately gave me my own seeds of interest.

This material helped me to become a retreat leader, writer, and speaker. I'm so glad I was "alert to life" even though I was bogged down with military functions, scouts, car pools, ballet classes, art classes, and other responsibilities associated with motherhood. I have the best of both worlds and the Golden Years are definitely the best!

Fill Your Personal Reservoir

By using this system for researching and organizing your material, you will constantly be filling your personal reservoir. It may be years before you are ready to speak or write on a specific topic, but when you are, you will have already done the research.

People often ask my mother and me how we can write a book so quickly. This chapter is a large part of the answer. We have spent years gathering the information. When we finally sit down to write the book, it is more a matter of putting it all together. We are not starting from scratch. We did that years ago. The topic is something that we have been filling ourselves with for a long time.

When we sat down to write the book *Raising Christians, Not Just Children,* we had over twenty years of my mother's research on raising children at our fingertips. She had started years ago with one folder labeled "Children." As she gathered more and more information, the files grew to include one on discipline, one on children and finances, one on adoption, one on family prayer time, and so forth.

As we wrote the book, we knew the basic areas we wanted to address and the order of the topics. The areas became the chapter headings and the order became the table of contents. We made a new file folder for each chapter. Since we are both visual-thinking Populars, we spread the file folders around us on the floor with the chapter titles written inside the open folders. We then took the files of years of research and placed them in the right chapter folders.

Since each article had been read, highlighted, and annotated earlier, we did not need to reinvest that time then. We just skimmed the notes and placed each article or note in the correct folder for the book. Then, one chapter at a time, we put the book together using notes, quotes, and articles. We spent a little over two weeks writing the book and it was one of our biggest at the time, over three hundred pages! But the work had been done passively over twenty years. Actually, you could say the book took more than twenty years to write, with most of the work being done in the last two weeks!

In addition to doing your research, this gathering of information can act as your personal survey of the public's interest on your topics. Magazines spend lots of money on research to determine what the magazine buying public wants to read. Every item placed on the valuable front cover space is there for a reason: their research indicates that topic will make you buy their magazine. Each article inside is there for the same reason: they believe that it is something of interest to the public. Keeping this in mind, what do you know if, after collecting articles for a year, one of your files has an inch worth of material and another is empty? One of your topics is hot, while the other is not something people want to know about now. Armed with that information, what should you do with that inch-thick file folder? Get it out. Review the articles and any additional notes you may have added and put your presentation on that topic together or write an article of your own. That topic's time has come!

Bonnie Skinner offers this advice: "If you are at a point where you feel caged in, continue to collect information on items that appeal to you. There *will* come a time when you will be glad you did!" Start gathering and organizing information on your seeds of interest today, even if you think it will be years before you begin to address that topic!

twelve

Putting Power Into
Your Presentation
∾
MARITA

We have looked at the various stages for preparing to give a speech or write a book or an article. You have examined your motives and expanded your topics. Armed with a variety of topics and a growing collection of research materials, which you have organized so you can find them, you are now ready to take these ideas and materials and put them together.

The concepts presented in this chapter will teach how to take a diverse selection of thoughts and ideas and bring them together to create a powerful presentation—either spoken or written—that will be easy for you to prepare and effectively communicate to the listener or reader. Actually sitting down and putting everything together is where many people get stuck. They have a few ideas they wish to communicate, but they do not know how to pull it all together.

Having these skills will be an asset to you no matter what you do in life, even if you never plan to give a speech. The book, *Business Protocol: How to Survive and Succeed in Business,* quotes a manager: "People who can express themselves clearly are at an advantage.... This goes beyond using good grammar, proper spelling and appropriate diction in all your communications; you must also speak and write to the point."[1]

There are five parts to putting power into your presentation. These steps will make it easy for you to pull it all together and make it easier for your audience to get your message and remember the key ideas you wish to communicate.

Passion

Many people think being a speaker looks like fun or they think it looks like a glamorous lifestyle. They ask, "How can I become a speaker?" I believe you don't really become a speaker; rather, it is an evolution. You don't one day decide, "I'd like to be a speaker" and then check out books, learn jokes, use other people's material, and reprocess it all into a speech you call your own. Some people do try this approach. Some may have excellent acting skills and be able to pull this off, but for most their message is empty. You can tell when you listen to these people that something doesn't ring true. You can probably think of people you have heard who have done this. You can learn everything else, but you cannot learn the passion.

Start by examining your own life. What are you so excited about that you can't keep quiet? What has God done in your life lately that you want to share? These are your passions. They are things that are a natural outpouring of who you are and what you believe. Your passions should be reflected in the seeds of interest you checked off in chapter ten. When you start with a passion, the other important pieces fall into place much more easily. Glenna Salsbury, president of the National Speakers Association, advises, "Your purpose should be larger than your speaking career. Speaking should be a vehicle to fulfill your purpose. Every time you give a presentation, is it springing from your purpose? If so, you are unforgettable on the platform."

Personal Examples

I have been involved in teaching others to be more effective speakers for many years. When I observe a speaker who is nervous or struggling, I want to go hold her hand. I have seen countless speakers who start out nervously, fidgeting with a pen or the change in their pocket and peppering their sentences with "and ahs." As I watch, hurting for the presenter, I have discovered an almost universal cure for the pain—both mine and the speaker's. As soon as the speaker begins to share a personal story, something she knows backward and forward, something she doesn't need notes to tell, she warms up. Speakers become more natural and animated as they tell stories from their own lives.

Personal examples add energy to your presentation. They let the audience know you have been there and that you know what you are talking about. Be sure to use them liberally throughout your presentation.

Preparation

Passion and personal examples are valuable tools, but if you don't prepare, you may gush on enthusiastically with no real point or purpose. The key to preparation is to know your subject well, know what ideas you wish to communicate, but yet be flexible enough to adjust some of your material to fit the specific needs of each group and the required time frame. When I was first beginning to speak publicly, my mother told me I should have ten hours of information in my head for every one hour I was going to speak. While that may be a bit extreme, it does insure that you *do* know your subject well!

Many novice speakers are afraid that, when they stand up in front of all those people, their minds will go blank. As a result, they write out their speeches word for word. When they stand up front they actually read the entire message. Most likely you have heard some of these speakers. It is obvious when someone is reading a speech. I always feel offended that I took my time to attend a program where the speaker is reading a speech. I feel as if they could have just mailed out the script and I could have done something else with my time.

Instead, what I am suggesting in preparing your speech is a method which will allow you to have everything you need in front of you, in case your mind goes blank, yet offers that flexibility. Notice the term "preparing a presentation" rather than "writing." A good speech should not be written out word for word. It should be "prepared" with all of the key ideas, teaching, stories, and Scripture in the notes, all of which you follow for continuity. But, by not writing it out word for word, you allow for flexibility in timing, group makeup, and the leading of the Holy Spirit as to the needs of this particular group.

The PIER system allows for all of these factors. PIER is an acronym for Point, Instruction, Example, and Reference. Think of yourself standing in front of an audience. You look out at them and they are looking back at you like a sea of faces.

The goal is to make your presentation stick out in their minds like a PIER sticks out into the ocean. By remembering "Point, Instruction, Example, Reference," the speaker can be assured that all the ingredients needed for an effective presentation are available, but they are arranged to allow for flexibility.

Betsy Jabola, a speaker and ventriloquist, uses this method for a variety of presentations. "Over the past five or six years, whenever I do a program for Sabbath school, children's stories, chapels, even banquets and bridal showers, I always use the PIER format. I start out with the main Point in mind, and develop stories (using the puppets with ventriloquism, etc.), and find songs, object lessons, and games that serve as examples and instruction with lots of good reference to back the program up.

"When I do a children's story in church, I take the main Point of the pastor's sermon and then develop a story using the puppets to illustrate as an Example and always end with the Instruction and Reference (in this case, the Bible).

"Whenever I have helped other people come up with programs for Sabbath school, I always use this acronym and show them how they can come up with their own program with confidence next time. I've taught in Sabbath school for eighteen years and have helped a lot of people get started learning how to put together programs when they feel panicked. PIER is an invaluable tool."

1. Point
As you begin your speech preparation, start with the main ideas you wish to convey to your audience. These ideas become your Points which, when collected together, become

the main points of your outline. As you sit down to prepare your presentation, say to yourself, "What are the key things I want the audience to remember?" Let's say you get three ideas. Take three separate pieces of paper and write one idea across the top of each. At this place in your preparation, your ideas may come to you in the form of a question, a single word, a thought, or a complete sentence. Don't worry about that yet. Simply write down the ideas as they come into your head.

Since you are writing each point on a separate piece of paper, it doesn't even matter if they are in the order in which you will ultimately use them. Often, once you get into your preparation, you may decide that the point you had as the first one should be somewhere else. Since they are on separate pieces of paper, you can just rearrange them as you see fit. These ideas become your Points, the *P* of the PIER.

About two inches down from each point, write an *I* in the margin of the paper. Another two inches down, write *E*, and another two inches, an *R*. This creates a simple "fill-in-the-blanks" form for your speech preparation.

Patty Lauterjung used the PIER formula this way. "One month after attending the CLASSeminar, I had to prepare a speech for Toastmasters on the topic of Speaking to Entertain. The goal was to entertain the audience through the use of humor drawn from personal experience and other material.

"My Perfect personality found it hard to think of myself as entertaining. It was difficult for me to even start the speech. I knew, however, most professional speakers use humor. I was determined to learn how to entertain people, knowing it would help my husband's and my financial seminar business.

Talking about budgets, goals, and debt can be very boring!

"As I sat brainstorming with my husband, Paul, about my speech, the PIER outline suddenly came to mind. We came up with the Point: frustrations of grocery shopping. My speech started, 'What is it that really irritates you about grocery shopping?' I then made a list of every Example I could think of from waiting in line to clipping coupons. Making decisions about what to buy jumped off the page at me, and I titled my speech 'Zillions of Choices.' I later changed it to 'Gripes of a Grouchy Grocery Shopper.'

"The References and Examples added body to the speech. Building stories around tissue and toothpaste drew the audience in by helping them relate to my experiences. A quote about toilet paper from Andy Rooney of *60 Minutes* brought the house down and my speech to a climax. It ended with three points of Instruction summarizing how to effectively handle choices.

"Not only did PIER help me prepare a speech, I actually won both a local and a divisional Toastmasters Humorous Speech contest and had fun in the process! I recommend using PIER to break 'writer's block' for you Perfects. The other personalities will benefit from the organization PIER brings to your ideas."

2. Instruction

Think about your Point. How are the listeners going to make that concept a part of their lives? These ideas become your instruction. For example, in your Point you may tell your audience that having a good prayer life is important. In the Instruction you will offer them several ways to improve their prayer life. Next to the *I* on your paper, write down the main techniques you want the audience to learn. Since these ideas are from your head and should be something you have studied or experienced, they will be concepts you know well. Therefore, you don't have to write out long, cumbersome instructions. By listing just the key steps, you can glance at your notes and be reminded of the things you intend to communicate. In this way you can be sure to include all the concepts while you are standing in front of the audience.

Depending on the time allowed for the presentation, you may give detailed instruction and even have the audience try your suggestions right there, or you may simply give them the techniques to implement your ideas. Offering listeners an idea without equipping them to accomplish it, will be frustrating to the audience and futile for you.

3. Example

If you give the listeners a point and then tell them how to do it but quit there, you may come across as preachy and hard to relate to. To show the audience that you know what you're talking about, that you've been there, include a personal story that exemplifies the principle. You may share your own struggle with the situation and show how you overcame it, or the example given may be that of a friend or family member. People remember stories better than just points. Again, these stories are usually things you have experienced, so you won't need to write them out word for word. Next to the *E* on your notes, jot down a few key words to remind you which stories you intend to tell with that point. If you have a lot of time, you may want to include several stories to make your point. Or, if your time is cut at the last minute, which often happens, you can pare your stories down and just tell one or even use an abbreviated version, if necessary. You can also adjust your stories so they are appropriate for the particular audience you are addressing at the time. If the group is made up of men and women, be sure to use stories that will relate to both. If it is all women, you may use slightly different examples. They will feel as though you customized the presentation just for them. The stories will give your points life!

4. Reference

So far all we have discussed are your own ideas. The Reference allows you to back up what you are saying and give it more authority. If your presentation is being given to a Christian audience, it should include various Scripture passages. These will be your references. You may have one verse you will want to quote or even several that will validate your point. Next to the *R* on your notes, list the location of the verse or verses you wish to use. If you are only using a couple of verses, you may want to write them out completely in your notes, so that you can quote them without having to fumble through your Bible while you are up front. If your time is cut, you can simply offer the audience the chapter and verse of the passage you are using and paraphrase it to save time. If you have been asked to stretch your message, which does occasionally happen, you can ask someone from the audience to find the verse and read it to the group.

In addition to the Bible, there are many other references you can use to reinforce what you are saying. They may include newspaper or magazine articles and books. This is how you will incorporate all the items you have been collecting in your file folders. When you quote from a magazine article, have the actual article in your hand and read from it. The visual stimulation adds variety for the audience and affirms your source. If you have collected the articles with the cover, as suggested in the previous chapter, show the cover briefly as you read the article. If your eyesight is such that reading the fine print while you are standing in front of a group is difficult, write the quote on a large sticky note and place it inside the magazine cover so you still have the appearance of reading the actual article.

Additionally, statistics or quotes from notable people work well here and add variety. I recommend that every speaker have a good quote book such as *Bartlett's Familiar Quotations* in their resource library. When you do use these additional references, be sure to list their source in your notes. You don't have to include the source in the verbal presentation, but you should have it in case anyone questions its validity.

After you have "filled in all your blanks," the next step is to make your points easier to remember. You as the speaker will have notes from which to work. Therefore you could give your presentation with one point being a question, another being a single word, and another being a thought. However, when there is no continuity between your points they are not as clear for your audience to catch or as easy for them to remember. Once the hard part is done, you are ready to clean it up.

Go back over your points. If, for example, three are questions and one is a single word, can you rework the idea the single word represents into a question so the points are uniform? Or, if there is no obvious pattern to your points, try to boil the points down to one or two words that represent the main thought. Review your points again. Do several of them start with the same letter? Do a couple of them rhyme? Or, can you use the first letters to spell a word that summarizes your overall message? If you see an emerging pattern, try to make the wording of the other points fit that pattern. This is where a thesaurus or a synonym finder is helpful. If you have one or two words that don't fit the pattern, look them up and see if you can find a synonym that will communicate the same point but fit within your pattern.

For example, here are three real points I often use to teach this concept. These points originally came from an article on father-daughter relationships by Gary Smalley.[2] His points are: (1) A father should include meaningful touching as his daughter grows up. (2) A father who wants to develop a close relationship with his daughter should invest himself in her best interest. (3) A father should keep his anger under control.

Now quickly cover up that paragraph and try to repeat those points without looking. You can't, can you? While those are three excellent points, they are too long and cumbersome to be easily remembered. Let's look at the first point. Can you condense it down to one key word? How about "Touch"?

Now let's look at the second point. There are several key words you could pick out, but since the word we have chosen for the first point begins with a *T*, can you think of a *T* word which captures the heart of that point? How about "Time"?

Okay, we've arrived at the last point. What *T* word comes to mind for this one? Most people come up with "Temper." It does capture the essence of the point, but does it work? Check your points once you have simplified them; they should all be the same parts of speech. They should be all nouns, all verbs, all thoughts, all sentences, or all questions. To check this you can simply put a prefix before the point. You might say, "A daughter needs Touch." "A daughter needs Time." Those both work. Point number three, "A daughter needs Temper." How can you rework that so that it fits the context, is a *T* word, and is the correct part of speech? Try, "A daughter needs Tenderness." Now you have three easy-to-remember points—Touch, Time, and Tenderness. The message is the same, but now it is also easy to remember!

The same basic concepts work for writing as well. If you think about PIER and chapters of this book, you will see the four parts used. Laura Riley told me how PIER had helped her writing. "Although an accomplished author, I attended the CLASSeminar to fine-tune my writing skills and learn how to successfully break into a speaking ministry. Learning the concept of PIER has improved both my writing and speaking abilities immeasurably. When I attended the CLASSeminar, I had just finished a devotional book and shortly after, received a contract with a publisher, which required that I do some editing—meaning shortening the length of the book! Since I am a Popular, I tend to be very wordy and before I went to the CLASSeminar I didn't know what to cut from my manuscript, fearing that deleting any of the words would take away some of the meaning. Implementing PIER as I edited changed everything. It was easy to see what was necessary to drive home a point, and what was just 'fluff.' I have learned to get my point across in my writing with fewer words and more impact. In addition, before attending the CLASSeminar I had been a guest speaker at only a few women's functions. I remember feeling very frustrated when trying to prepare for these engagements, not knowing how to put together a meaningful presentation that could be easily followed and enjoyed. I seemed to go off on many tangents. Again, PIER turned my anxiety into accomplishment. Now, when I prepare a talk, I have a pattern that has purpose and meaning. The audience stays interested, and I am in the process of launching a speaking ministry with new confidence!"

Presentation

Once you have filled out your "form" using the PIER formula, you have your speech basically prepared. When you are ready to actually present your message, you will need an opening, which may be a story—the *E* in PIER—which will put you at ease. Or, it may be a question that helps to create a need in the audience for your subject. If you do begin with a question, be sure that it is a question with an obvious answer, and one that everyone present can answer affirmatively, without embarrassment. This same principle is true for all questions you might ask throughout the presentation.

I was recently sharing the platform with a speaker who asked the audience lots of questions. But, because she had not set them up by making the answers clear, the exercise was painfully flat. Additionally, questions to which you want the audience members to stand up and share a lengthy answer are best used in a workshop setting, not a keynote presentation.

When I begin one of my presentations, I always ask the

audience, "How many of you have noticed there are people out there who are different from you?" Of course everyone has noticed that. So they can all answer by raising their hands in agreement. To indicate that I am expecting a response to the question, in particular a raised hand, I raise my hand as I lean into the audience and ask the question. By asking a question to which they can all respond, I have already done several things. First, I have created an atmosphere of interaction. Rather than having a sense of being preached at, the audience is already involved. Additionally, since the question is something that applies to everyone, the communal response draws the audience together.

After your opening story, question or questions, move right into your points. Remember, PIER is a formula, not usually an outline in itself. However, as Patty Lauterjung shared, if the speech only has one point, PIER could become your outline. By preparing your presentation using PIER you have all the information you need. But when you actually present it, you can start with (the Example)—the story—and then move into the Point you learned from the story, then teach the audience how to apply that in their own lives—(the Instruction), and then wrap up that point with a quote or Scripture. You can arrange the Point, Instruction, Example, and Reference any way you want and you can present it differently each time. In the earlier example from Patty Lauterjung, she started with the Point, added the Examples, her quote from Andy Rooney was the Reference, and she closed with the Instruction. This flexibility allows each presentation to be unique, fresh, and specifically applicable to each audience.

If you choose to use a handout for your presentation, which

I suggest because it allows your audience to follow along and provides them with a place to take notes, use the Points of your outline to make up your handout. If you are using Scripture passages or quotes, you may also want to include them in a smaller font with the key points. This prevents losing people as they lean over to the person next to them and ask, "What verse was that?" By including the chapter and verses on the handout, you can skip them in a really tight time situation, but still allow the people to have that valuable part of your presentation. However, be a pro. Do not tell the audience your time has been cut, or that you are out of time; simply say something like, "I have included some special Bible verses on your handout for you to use as a study guide when you get home." That way it looks like you had planned it that way all along!

If you do choose to use a handout, be sure to include your name, address, and phone number to identify whose material the audience is taking home. This way, if they want to quote you at a later date or use your ideas in some research of their own, they know how to find you to get permission. Plus, if they love what you said and want to recommend you to another group, they will know how to contact you.

Finally, you will need a closing, which may include a recapping or a summary of your points and end with a challenge or call to commitment. Often a poem or other inspirational piece that exemplifies your message is an effective closing. (If the closing quote or poem is not original, be sure to cite the source.)

Many people who are giving a Christian message in a church or church-related setting feel that they should close with prayer. Unless the presentation is an actual sermon, I suggest that you not use a prayer as your final words. Closing with a prayer in a non-church service setting confuses the audience. In our society, the way we show appreciation to a person who is on the "stage"—a performer, singer, or speaker—is by applause. This lets you know you did a good job and is the audience's way of thanking you. However, closing in prayer creates a somber and quiet mood. We are not accustomed to breaking into applause at the sound of "Amen." So when you close with prayer, the audience doesn't know whether they should thank you with applause or keep quiet. It creates an awkward and uncomfortable moment for everyone.

If a prayer of confession or commitment is appropriate after your presentation, there are two effective ways to handle it. One is to have the emcee or program chairman do it after you have finished. Or, you can offer the prayer that is on your heart. But then come back with your summary of points, closing poem, or concluding challenge. This provides an effective transition from the prayer mood to a powerful closing and will leave your audiences on an up note.

Occasionally, the desired mood may be a quiet, somber exit into a time of reflection or stillness. In such circumstances, the prayer may be the most effective way to close.

If everything goes as expected, you should now have a perfect presentation. However, perfection is seldom a part of a speaker's world. There are too many variables. The speaker or singer before you can take too long. The food service can be late. The entire program may have started late. While the speaker is usually the one the people have come to hear and the one the meeting planner has built the entire program

around, they are usually last on the schedule. All of the tardiness of the other parts of the program now become the
speaker's problem. Do you take all of your time and have the
meeting end late, or do you finish on time?

In cases like that, speaker Marilyn Heavilin asks the meeting
planner, "Do you want what you paid for, or do you want me
to be done on time?" Phrasing it that way helps put it in perspective. Sometimes they say, "Take all the time you need."
Other times, they do need to be out of the room by a certain
time and they need you to trim.

If you write your speech out word for word, you will be in
trouble. I am sure that you have heard speakers whose time
had been cut who gave as much of their presentation as they
had time for and then said, "Well, we are out of time. If you
want to hear the rest of the message, you'll have to buy the
book." Or, "You'll have to buy the tape." Have you ever
heard that? How does it make you feel? I feel cheated. I have
taken my time, and paid my money to hear a professional
speaker. I want to hear the whole thing.

If you have prepared your speech using the PIER formula,
you can be flexible. If you are using handouts with the
Scripture passages on them, you can easily cut them from the
spoken presentation. You can delete the magazine articles you
were going to refer to. You can trim the number of stories you
tell and even skip them totally on some points. Since your
handout has all of the points listed, you do not want to skip
any of them, and the instructions are important. You can easily
cut your speech in half without the audience ever knowing!

One time I was the first keynote speaker of the day. The day
was packed. Several other keynote speakers were scheduled

throughout the day, as well as different workshops and lunch. There were hundreds of people in attendance and only fifteen minutes allotted between the general sessions and the workshops—which were held in different buildings. I was scheduled to have an hour for my session. However, as often happens, the program got started late. By the time I got onstage, the program was already twenty minutes behind. Even though I had planned for an hour, I smiled and said, "I will get you back on schedule."

The audience had the handout. I trimmed my opening story way down, shortened the stories I'd planned to use to illustrate each point, and did not use every Bible passage I had intended. I was done just two minutes after the time I was supposed to have been done in the first place! I was the hero of the day because I had brought them back on schedule without anyone in the audience ever knowing there was a problem.

Additionally, PIER more easily allows for the Holy Spirit's direction based on the needs of the group. If the speech is written out word for word, and you feel a prompting to make a shift, it is hard to do. You worry about how to add it in and how to get back on track. When you have prepared your speech rather than writing it out, you can have variations without stress. Sometimes I find myself saying words that I had not intended to say or sharing a story that was not in my notes. As the words are coming out of my mouth, part of my brain is saying, "Where did that come from? That is not what I usually say here." Almost always, someone comes up to me afterward and says, "You know what you said about _____? You said that for me. It was just what I needed to hear today." Thank you, Holy Spirit!

Practice

The final thing you need to do is practice. Once you have found the subject area of your passion, peppered it with the vitality of personal examples, prepared your message, and gotten the presentation together, you are ready to practice. Start alone in your bedroom or office, preferably in front of a full-length mirror. Allow that passion to show and use hand gestures to clarify your points. I suggest that the gestures you use be specifically tied to the words being spoken at that time. Any time you use a number in your speech, hold up that number of fingers. If you say something like, "she spoke so softly, I could hardly hear her," hold your hand up to your ear. I have found that if you pretend that the audience is deaf, and that they are reading your lips, you will use your hands to attempt to aid them in their understanding. By doing this you create effective gestures that will replace a distracting or repetitive chopping motions.

Work on your message until you are comfortable with all the parts. Then tape-record it. Listen to how you sound. You are apt to find places where you have lots of gap fillers such as "ah" and "you know." These usually indicate an area where you are not as familiar with your material or are not comfortable with it. Make changes or study those areas more completely. While it is unlikely you will ever be completely happy with your finished product, the next thing is to give your speech in front of supportive, but honest friends or family. This may be three people in your living room, or it may be your Bible study group at your church. Ask for their encouragement and insight; notice that I didn't say criticism. Accept

their praise and listen to their suggestions. If they have suggested many changes, you may want to give your speech once
more in a controlled environment before you venture beyond
the safety of your support network. If they give you a thumbs-
up, go on. Share what God has put on your heart with others
and expect results!

When you prepare your speech using the PIER system you
can be confident that you have included everything you need
for a strong presentation and still have the freedom and flexibility that is the sign of a "pro"!

thirteen

Christian Leadership Out in the World

∾

FLORENCE

Do you hear the call of the Lord asking you to communicate effectively and lovingly in a secular setting? Should a Christian be a leader in a social, civic, or business environment? Should we attempt to be quiet witnesses in a noisy world? How do we know if God wants us to minister outside of the local church?

In my thirty years of Christian ministry I have served in a leadership capacity in the local church, in the business world, and in a variety of secular social and civic organizations. Through these experiences I have developed some basic guidelines to answer these questions.

1. Check with the Lord

From the beginning, Fred and I have been open to the Lord's leading, knowing that as we kept in touch with the Lord in prayer and questions, he would provide answers. Although it is wise to seek others' opinions before taking on responsibility in any group, the Lord Jesus is the only one with the power to open and shut doors. He can give us the excitement to move ahead or the check in our spirit that sends doubt to our mind. As with any relationship, we must keep in close touch with the

Lord in order to know his will. If we only shoot up emergency prayers in time of crisis, we can't be sure we will know whether it is the Lord speaking or the world giving answers.

When Fred and I were first on staff at Campus Crusade for Christ, Vonette Bright invited me to join the Women's Club. This was part of the Federated Women's Club of America, a social-civic group who majored in good works for the community. Vonette was third vice-president in charge of membership and, when her term ran out, she suggested that I be her successor. The society ladies were wary of Campus Crusade. They looked at the massive hotel headquarters on the hill as something akin to a monastery and were afraid Vonette and I were trying to infiltrate the group for subversive purposes. In addition to these fears, the group was inbred with long-term local society residents and was not seeking outsiders from the East to step into leadership. When my nomination for third vice-president was announced, I received unsigned letters telling me to withdraw. One stated, "Even the Lord Jesus had to die before He ascended to the throne." These letters were enough to deter the fainthearted, but I brought the question to the Lord. "If you are telling me to withdraw, make it clear and keep this problem before me. If these are roadblocks from the enemy, remove the concern and inspire me to move on." As I prayed this I relaxed and waited for the Lord's response. I did not call anyone and try to drum up support. I didn't ask around to find out who wrote these discouraging words, nor did I complain about these letters to anyone.

As days went by I felt peace about quietly moving on. I had caused no fuss, stirred up no warring sides, and was elected without opposition. Within a few months the second vice-president became ill and resigned and the first vice-president's husband was transferred out of town. I was suddenly the first vice-president, with the bylaws stating I must become president the next year. Doesn't the Lord have a sense of humor?!

2. Look to your past experiences

Where have you been successful? Where have you met defeat? These are the questions I ask when others come to me with desires for ministry. The answers often provide obvious direction. "I tried to start support groups three times, but nobody came." This doesn't mean she is a bad person but it at least indicates this church isn't interested in support groups at this time.

"The pastor asked me to write a couples' Bible study but when I asked when I would start teaching it, he told me I wouldn't be the teacher, I would only write it. They would find a man to teach my material." This church is not ready for female leadership. Move on.

In our case Fred and I were asked to teach adult Sunday school. We set to work and wrote a course that built up in numbers quite quickly. We put ads in the paper and had parties at our own expense. After four terms of enthusiastic response, the class that we had intended to teach forever was dropped from the listings. We found out much later that the pastor feared his church was becoming known for us and not for him. This scenario was repeated in another setting and we learned that the local church was not where we belonged. We started teaching the same material in our home, where our children sat and listened each Friday night. We trained leaders to handle the small groups that soon grew beyond our capacity. We enlisted the help of unchurched neighbors who allowed us to use their family rooms. Through their listening to the teaching, each family became believing Christians and many lives were changed. From these home classes, we branched out to week-end retreats for couples and the material ultimately became our book *After Every Wedding Comes a Marriage.*

Check with the Lord first and then see what works and what doesn't. In any leadership position it is important to remember *not* to take every defeat as a personal rejection. This may be the wrong place at the wrong time.

3. Don't play Winnie Witness

I have a Jewish friend who owns a speakers' bureau. One day he said to me, "I never book Christian speakers for secular groups." When I asked why, he replied, "You can't trust them." He then explained that Christians feel they must evangelize every group they go to even when they are asked to give a purely motivational talk. "You can't trust them."

I want to be trusted. I must decide before going to speak whether I'm willing to be true to the call or not. I'm not to turn each business luncheon into a tent meeting. If I don't want to give a business talk, I shouldn't accept the engagement.

The reason I was successful as president of the Women's Club in spite of their fears was that I did not bring religion into the general meetings. I was true to the position.

In my book *How To Get Along With Difficult People,* I have a character called Winnie Witness. I invented her from a Women's Club member who was so evangelistic that she wouldn't give her credit card to the gas station attendant until she went through the Four Spiritual Laws with her. I tried to tone her down, but she felt "called of the Lord" to bring everyone she met to their knees in repentance.

I cast her as Winnie Witness in the skit I put on at the Club and gave her the admonition to love people and not try to beat them into the kingdom. When the skit was over and we lined up on the stage to have our pictures taken for the local newspaper, we couldn't find her or the photographer. She had him pinned against the men's room door and was already on Law Three! She never did get the point, and when the ladies of the Club saw her coming, they fled in the opposite direction. She meant well but she turned everyone off with her insensitive witnessing. To minister in a social setting we must live our Christian life so effectively that people see a difference in us and want to know what it is. We can't turn the monthly meeting into an altar call! Then what can we do?

4. Read the bylaws

Every civic-social group of any size has bylaws. These were written years ago and no one has any idea what they say. Before taking any leadership position, ask to read them. When I read the bylaws for the Federated Women's Club, I found a section admonishing us to lift the spiritual values of our members. When I became president, I brought this item before the board and asked permission to reactivate the dormant "Religion Section." This was no threat, in that it was voluntary and no one had to go. To keep within the rules, we had to charge and make our Bible studies a "Special Project."

It's always important in a secular group to know the boundaries and stay within them. As I taught the Bible study, the group grew and flourished and it was exciting to realize that I was the only person they knew who showed them that Scripture had meaning for everyday life. Since they came from liberal churches or none at all, I was assured that, if I hadn't taught it, they wouldn't know it. Women were coming to the Lord and lives were being changed, all without my being religious at the general meetings. People who hadn't been around for a year or two came back and said, "There's something different here. Everyone seems nicer."

Soon we started a yearly prayer breakfast. At first the general members were wary and afraid they'd have to pray. But as all had excellent speakers and musicians, the attendance grew.

As other women's clubs heard of our success in spiritual values, they asked if I'd start Bible studies for them. I brought in teachers I'd trained to help and then the district convention decided to have a prayer breakfast. It was at that point that the state gave me a special award for outstanding work in lifting the spiritual values of our members, and the next year they started a prayer breakfast at the state convention. Within a few years the success of the breakfasts in California spread and the Federated Women's Clubs of America sponsored a prayer breakfast at the national convention.

How grateful I am that I brought my concerns to the Lord when I received those anonymous letters telling me to withdraw. Throughout the years so many were blessed and some of the ladies identified themselves and told me they were sorry they had written in haste without even knowing me.

We are called to be beacons in a dim world. The verses I used for my two terms as president were Philippians 2:14-15, "Do all things without murmuring or disputing, that you may become blameless and harmless, children of God without fault, in the midst of a crooked and perverse generation among whom you shine as lights in the world" (NKJV).

5. Have a servant's attitude

In James 3:1 we are told that few of us should be teachers of the Word, for we will be judged more harshly than the rest. Surely, I learned this lesson personally as I became "The Bible teacher lady" in the Women's Club. Some were afraid I'd try to make them join Campus Crusade. Others thought I'd make them feel guilty or that I'd be "too holy" and untouchable. I made sure I diffused all their fears by never mentioning any church or group and repeating often that we were there to let the Lord change our individual lives, not to join anything. I always gave more than was expected of me and let them all know right from the beginning that I was willing to work in the kitchen, clear tables, or sell tickets. Word got around that I was one of the group and didn't think I was too good to help others. Had I presented a lofty attitude or looked down on those who weren't spiritual, I would have been out of there at the next election.

In 1 Kings 12:7, when Rehoboam came to his father Solomon's advisors and asked how to be a good king, they told him to speak kindly to all, answer all who asked him a question, and have the attitude of a servant. I took this advice personally.

Are you considering possible leadership in a secular group? It can be a rewarding ministry if you check with the Lord and wait upon his Spirit to give you a feeling of assurance. If you look to your own talents and past experiences before taking on a position of leadership ... if you don't charge in like Winnie Witness and turn them all off ... if you check the bylaws and make sure you're not breaking any rules ... if you have a humble attitude and do the very best you can in any set of circumstances—you too can be a light in the midst of a crooked and perverse nation.

Do you hear the call of the Lord asking you to communicate effectively and lovingly in a secular setting? As Samuel answered, "Here am I, Lord. Send me!"

appendix

Dressing for the Platform
∾
MARITA

Your appearance is important, and it reflects a sense of confidence, or a lack of it, and an air of credibility. Someone whose clothing is out of date, worn, dirty, or poorly coordinated implies that the message may be the same: out of date and invalid.

Some people are naturally gifted speakers, and others have to work at it. Likewise, some people look great no matter what they wear, while others struggle with even the most basic outfits. However, those with little closet coordination can learn some basic principles that transcend trends and allow them the confidence needed in front of an audience. I developed some concepts years ago when I was working as a professional color consultant. The majority of my clients were in the less coordinated category—the ones who needed help and knew it. I would spend a couple hours with them, selecting the correct colors and advising them how to use their colors. Yet, when I saw them later, usually wearing their colors, something still wasn't quite right.

After eight years as a professional color consultant, I came to the following conclusion: You are better off wearing the wrong colors right, than wearing the right colors wrong. If you are going to have only one part right, putting things together correctly is more important than wearing the correct colors.

While I no longer do color consulting, I still enjoy teaching wardrobe coordination techniques. I call these ideas "Looking Your Best Without Spending the Most." While fashion trends come and go, these guidelines will work season after season, year after year. If you choose to ignore these rules for a current or trendy look, just remember to go back to them when that outfit is passé. Looking good is a matter of knowing how to put things together.

My stage clothing has developed its own persona. I have learned that the audience responds best to me when I wear clothing that is dramatic, bold, and different. People repeatedly make enthusiastic comments like, "That outfit is *you!*" They feel the clothing is me because my speaking style is dramatic and bold.

I have shared the platform many times with Donna Partow and Sherry Rose Shepherd. Donna comes from a Middle Eastern and French background. She has an olive complexion, high cheekbones, beautiful, big brown eyes, and smooth, thick, dark hair. Sherry Rose, a former beauty queen, is perfectly proportioned with blue eyes, blonde hair, and a cute little turned-up nose. Recently Donna came to one of our conferences. When it was time for her to give her speech she appeared, wonderfully dressed in a bright fuchsia pantsuit with rhinestones scattered along the front of the jacket. Donna asked me, "Is this me?" Unsure of what to say, but being an honest-to-a-fault type of person, I wrinkled up my nose slightly. She said, "Sherry gave it to me," which explained everything. The outfit looked like Sherry, but it was just too "fou fou" for Donna. Donna's coloring is exotic and her speaking style is strong. I suggested that she should get a few things for the platform that were darker, dramatic, and exotic.

Donna and I spoke together a month or so later. She had on a smashing outfit which was *her.* It was a one-piece black pantsuit, with metallic gold trim along the shoulders and waist. On her it was stunning and complimented her style.

I have learned that, for the stage, wearing clothing that fits you, your style, and your presentation is more important than the exact colors. Take your personality into consideration as you shop.

If you are a Popular personality, look for brighter colors, unique styles, and clothing that has a "costume" feeling. Wear larger earrings, and necklaces that fit the theme of the outfit. Shoes and hosiery should be colorful, matching the outfit.

If you are a Powerful personality, shop for bright colors and simple, large prints in clean-lined styles. Jewelry should be bold and make a statement. Do not simply put on the same little gold chain with everything—which is the inclination of most Powerfuls. Instead, use a wide gold choker or a dramatic pin. Keep both clothing and jewelry clean and simple. Remember, you want to make a statement.

If you are a Perfect personality, aim for elegance and simplicity in traditional and classic styles. Build on basic colors such as black, navy, gray, burgundy, and royal blue with red or yellow for a bit of drama. Antique jewelry will work well, as will basics such as pearls. Depending on your coloring, light/dark contrasting outfits can be a good choice. Many Perfect women, especially if their topic and presentation style is emotional or sensitive, like a Victorian touch in their clothing.

For the Peaceful, an unstructured look with flowing fabrics is effective. Fabrics such as raw silk or a wrinkled gauze create the comfortable, relaxed feeling that fits the Peaceful's presentation style. Colors in the earthy and muted shades will work well. Aim to create an artsy look with distinctive hand-crafted jewelry. Be careful, however, that your clothing looks fresh and coordinated. It is easy to get so comfortable that you have the look of an unmade bed.

Regardless of your personality, it is important to put extra effort into dressing for the platform. The things that work on the stage may well be things that you would never wear to the store or office, as they would appear "too much." But on the stage, in front of an audience, you want to have a look that sets you apart and lends dignity to your work.

Hosiery and Shoes

When you want to create a polished, put-together first impression, pay extra attention to your hosiery. Colored pantyhose that complement the total image of your outfit will always provide a more complete look than nude, suntan, or other natural looking colors. The more casual, natural colors should be used with sportswear. While it is not wrong to wear them with dressier outfits, colors add something extra. If you wear colored pantyhose, use the following guidelines.

The color of your pantyhose and the color of your shoes should match. The two of them must be the same color as a major color in the bottom half of your outfit. For example, if you have a plaid skirt which is navy blue and white with a small stripe of yellow, you would not use yellow hose and shoes.

Assuming the white and navy are used in equal proportion, you could use either to accent. If it is winter, choose the navy. In summer, the all-white combination would be acceptable. If there are several equally major colors in the bottom half, look at the rest of your outfit and choose accordingly.

Regardless of the color, selecting shoes and pantyhose to match will give you a polished and formal look. With a pink outfit, use pink shoes and hose. With a plum outfit use plum, and use blue with a blue outfit. A current favorite outfit of mine is totally blue. The whole ensemble is so blue, I doubt I will wear it anywhere else, but it is a perfect stage outfit. An additional benefit of the monochrome look is that wearing the same color shoes, hosiery, and outfit is slimming for most figures and makes you look taller.

The exception to the matching pantyhose rule is when the outfit has light/dark contrast. In this case, carry that same quality into the shoes and hose. Use the dark color for the shoes, and the light for the hose. Do not reverse the order, as it draws too much attention to your the feet and makes them appear larger.

Using the same example of the plaid skirt with navy and white, you would attain a summery look by wearing white hose and navy shoes, not navy hose with white shoes. This combination gives a summery look. In the winter, you may wear the same outfit with navy shoes and hose. Other possibilities might include a cheerful summer dress of white and fuchsia with which you would wear white hose with fuchsia shoes. Or, with a red-trimmed off-white dress, use red shoes and off-white hose.

A light/dark contrast look may make legs look heavier and

tends to visually chop your body in half, making it a poor choice for short women. Keep these points in mind when making your own selections.

While having shoes to match every outfit may sound extravagant, it can be a "shoestring" selection. If you have more outfits that match fuchsia shoes than those that go with a "basic" beige shoe, the matching shoe will be the more economical choice. You can look your best without spending the most!

If you don't have colored shoes or you prefer the more natural shades, you can still make selections that will keep the feeling of the entire outfit intact. The natural shades include colors such as suntan, nude, taupe, gray, and coffee. If the total effect of the outfit is light, such as whites or pastels, use the lighter naturals such as nude or suntan. If the total look is more of a medium intensity, use either suntan or taupe hose. If the look is darker, use coffee or gray. If the outfit has warm tones such as off-rust or brown, use the coffee hose. If the outfit has cool tones such as blue, purple, or burgundy, use the gray.

When using natural-colored hose, shoes and hose do not have to match, but select shoes that are in keeping with the overall look of the outfit. For example, if you only have two pairs of dress shoes, white and black, use the white shoes with outfits whose primary effect is light, such as pastels and floral prints. Use the black shoes with darker outfits such as black, gray, navy, burgundy, or purple. However, never wear medium or dark hose with white shoes.

Regardless of the color of the pantyhose, use "sandalfoot" hose when wearing open-toed shoes. "Sandalfoot" means there are no obvious lines or changes of color in the toe area of the hose. Wearing "reinforced" toes with sandals or other open-toed shoes can ruin the look you have worked so hard to create.

In addition to the color, the right shoe styles are also important. Avoid wearing open-toed shoes or sandals with heavy clothes such as wools or corduroy. These thicker fabrics call for a more sturdy, closed shoe such as a basic pump or even boots. In the same way, avoid wearing a clunky looking pump with light-weight, airy fabrics or styles. If you are limited to one style of shoe for all year-round wear, a lighter looking pump, one with a more pointed toe and thinner heel of one to three inches, will be your best investment.

Undergarments

One area that is often overlooked in creating a smooth, put-together look is the area of undergarments: panties, bras, and slips. I am amazed at how often I see a woman whose clothing matches, shoes and purse are right, and jewelry accents the outfit well, but whose bra strap is showing or whose slip hangs out through the slit in her skirt. Inappropriate or mischosen underwear is a big image-wrecker! There is no way you can look your best with your underwear showing!

First, be sure that you have a bra that fits you well. You should have at least one low-cut bra in your lingerie wardrobe for blouses, sweaters, or dresses with low necklines. If you are wearing a blouse or sweater with a wide neckline such as a "tank top" or "boat neck," you may have trouble with your bra straps showing. The most efficient way to avoid this is to purchase some thin ribbon. Cut it into a piece about one inch long and tack the middle of it down to the shoulder seam on the shirt. Then sew a snap on each end of the ribbon. When you put the top on, simply snap the little straps you have made around the bra strap and the top will stay in place and keep the bra straps hidden.

The most common mistake women make with their slip is with slit slips and slit skirts. The problem is that the slit in the slip and the slit in the skirt never seem to slit in the same place at the same time. The solution to this problem is to get what is called a "petal" or "tulip" slip. On these slips, the slit is tapered so that it is more open at the hemline than it is at the top, creating a triangular shaped opening. By comparison, regular slit slips don't really have an opening at all, just a slit.

If you wear skirts with varied lengths, you may need at least two different slips, a long one and a short one. A slip provides two services. First, it keeps your skirt from sticking to your hose. Second, it blocks light from showing through your skirt. For both of these reasons, be sure that your slip length and your skirt length are close to one another.

As I watch women in airports, malls, and other public places, I see there is still a need to remind women about panty lines. If you are wearing a tight-fitting skirt or pair of slacks, there are two options. One is to wear pantyhose with no panties. Most pantyhose today are made with a cotton crotch and are designed to be worn as actual undergarments. If you are uncomfortable with this concept, try the pantyhose that are a solid color on the "panty" portion such as Hanes Underalls.

The other option is to wear full panties rather than "bikini" style. This way the edges of the panties do not cross your body at its fuller parts or the tighter areas on the clothing. Having wide lace edges on the panties will also help reduce panty lines.

Makeup and Jewelry

Whatever you have worked to achieve with your clothing, carry that same quality into your makeup and accessories. For example, if you are wearing a beautiful summer dress with pastel flowers in a soft fabric, with maybe a little lace, be sure your accessories complement that delicate look; wear pearls or a lightweight gold necklace. Avoid heavy chains or necklaces with large medallions. Likewise, your makeup should be soft: pastel colors, frosted eye shadow and lipstick, lightly applied.

On the other hand, if you are wearing a trendy outfit with bright colors and bold prints, you'll want jewelry that is heavier and larger in scale. Your makeup will need more color so you don't look washed out or overpowered by your clothing.

Remember, looking your best is not a matter of spending a lot of money, but rather knowing what to do with what you've got. By following these suggestions, you can be assured you are making the right choice.

A Few More Guidelines

Here are some commonsense reminders I have collected over the years:

- Aim for a polished, put-together look.
- Have a professional look on the job; save frills for after hours.

- Replace buttons if they aren't good quality. Plastic looking buttons can cheapen even an expensive suit.

- Don't overdo your makeup or your hairstyle. Be consistent in the image you want to convey.

- If you are short, it is better to stay with a single color. Breaking up the color line will tend to make you seem even shorter.

- Learn where the hemline of a jacket should hit your hips. Never stop a line at an obvious flaw in the body. (My favorite hint!)

- Don't choose corduroys unless you are thin.

- In deciding where to spend money, remember you will be viewed more from the waist up, so look for extra quality in blazers, jackets, blouses, and sweaters.

- Before leaving home, view yourself in a mirror from all angles.

- Start wearing the makeup that matches your skin tone and clothing.

- Begin to build your wardrobe around basics.

Whether you are at home, at work, traveling, doing something recreational, visiting with friends, or shopping, it takes so little to look your best. Take a few moments to "put yourself together" the best you can before leaving your home. When we are at home, it takes just a few extra moments to add some lipstick or comb your hair. By looking your best wherever you go, you are saying to others, "I care!" This kind of attitude builds others up, and it shows them they are worth looking your best for. When you are dressing for the platform, remember: you never have a second chance to make a good first impression!

notes

∾

ONE
Discovering Your Communication Personality

1. You can order *Personality Plus, Personality Puzzle,* and *Getting Along With Almost Anybody* by calling 1-800-433-6633.

THREE
Communicating Through Conversation

1. Michael Korda, *Signature,* September 1986.
2. Sarah Mahoney, "Hear Between the Lines," *Home Office Computing,* October 1997, 126.
3. Donna G. Kordela, "Small Talk: Chitchat that Leads to Serious Discussion," *Executive Female,* November/December 1985, 33.
4. Mahoney.
5. Mahoney.
6. *The Delany Sisters' Book of Everyday Wisdom,* quoted in *Good Housekeeping,* November 1994, 128.
7. *Executive Female,* May/June 1991.
8. Condensed from Roger Ailes, *You Are the Message* (Homewood, Ill.: Dow-Jones Irwin, 1988) in "Secrets of Successful Leaders," *Reader's Digest,* May 1988, 133.

FIVE
Be of Good Cheer: Compliments and Criticism

1. Taken from *It Takes So Little to Be Above Average* by Florence Littauer. Copyright 1996 by Harvest House Publishers, Eugene, Oregon, pages 57-61. Used by permission.

SIX
Effective Written Communication: The Paper Trail

1. Hermine Hartley, *The Family Book of Manners* (Uhrichsville, Ohio: Barbour, 1990), 147.
2. Robert Pampell and Steven G. Meilleur, "E-Mail Ethics," *Computer Scene,* October 1997, 12.

SEVEN
Written Communication: Digital Devices

1. Maryann Piotrowski, *Effective Business Writing* (New York: HarperPerennial, 1996), 104.
2. Deborah Dumaine, *The Vest Pocket Guide to Business Writing* (Englewood Cliffs, N.J.: Prentice Hall, 1997), 151.

NINE
The ABCs of Public Communication

1. Murray Stein, *Working Woman,* July 1995, 63.

ELEVEN
Researching and Organizing Your Topic

1. Patsy Clairmont, *Under His Wings* (Carmel, N.Y.: Guidepost Edition, 1994), 122-23.

TWELVE
Putting Power Into Your Presentation

1. Reviewed in "Book Summary," *Spirit Magazine,* January 1992, 22.
2. Gary Smalley, "Fathers and Daughters," *Fullness,* Mar/Apr. 1986, 24.

Booklets

The following booklets address issues of concern to those who are interested in more information or in becoming professional speakers. All booklets, with the exception of "Hear, Hear," are written by Marita Littauer.

Can I Earn A Living Speaking?
This booklet addresses some of the most frequently asked questions regarding setting fees as a speaker and developing a product table.

Promotional Materials for Christian Speakers
Writing promotional materials for yourself is difficult. This booklet offers step-by-step guidance for creating effective and cost-efficient promotional materials.

Helping Us Help You
Many speakers believe that a speakers' bureau will solve all their problems. This booklet explains how to work with a speakers' bureau and how to develop a positive relationship.

The Next Step
Once you have started speaking, what do you do next? The Next Step provides a blueprint for your speaking career so you know what step to take next.

Knowing Your Audience, written with Kristen Welch
When you speak to many different denominations, it is important to know how their beliefs may differ from yours. This booklet provides

an overview of the major denominations and their views on major issues.

Hear, Hear, by Jean Duckworth
Written by an audio-visual pro, this booklet offers specific advice for speakers to help them use microphones and audio-visual equipment correctly.

Additional books and tapes are available. Please call 800-433-6633 or visit the CLASS web site at www.classervices.com for a complete listing of available resources, prices, and ordering information.

Seminars

Improve your Speaking and Writing Skills at the CLASSeminar. Five seminars are held each year throughout the United States and Canada, usually one in the West, one in the East, and the remaining three in various parts of the country.

Please call **800-433-6633** to receive the complete CLASSeminar brochure or visit the CLASS web site at **www.classervices.com** for a current listing of seminar locations.